Christmas Songs
for Keyboard

Music arranged and processed by Barnes Music Engraving Ltd.,
East Sussex TN22 4HA, UK.

Published 1994

All I Want For Christmas Is My Two Front Teeth

Words & Music by Don Gardner

Suggested Registration: Trombone
Rhythm: Swing
Tempo: ♩ = 112

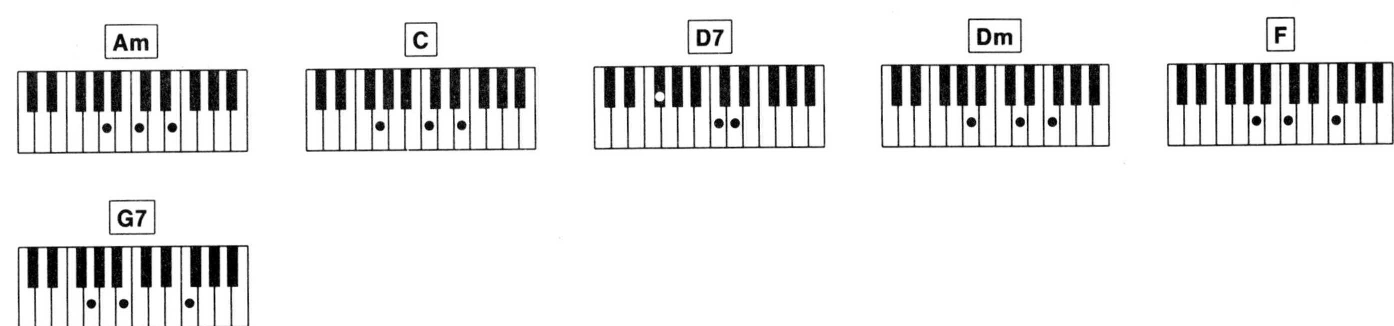

G7   C
two front teeth, see my two front teeth.   Gee, if I could on - ly have my
F   C   G7   C
two front teeth, then I could wish you 'Mer - ry Christ - mas.'
D7
All I want for Christ - mas is my two front teeth, my
G7   C
two front teeth, see my two front teeth.   Gee, if I could on - ly have my
F   C   G7   C
two front teeth, then I could wish you 'Mer - ry Christ - mas.'
Am   C   D7   Dm   F
G7

ANOTHER ROCK & ROLL CHRISTMAS

Words & Music by Leander, Seago and Glitter

Suggested Registration: Tenor Saxophone
Rhythm: Pop / Swing
Tempo: ♩ = 132

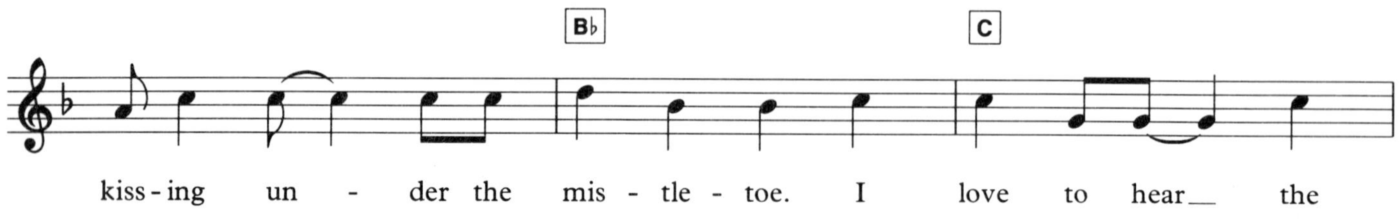

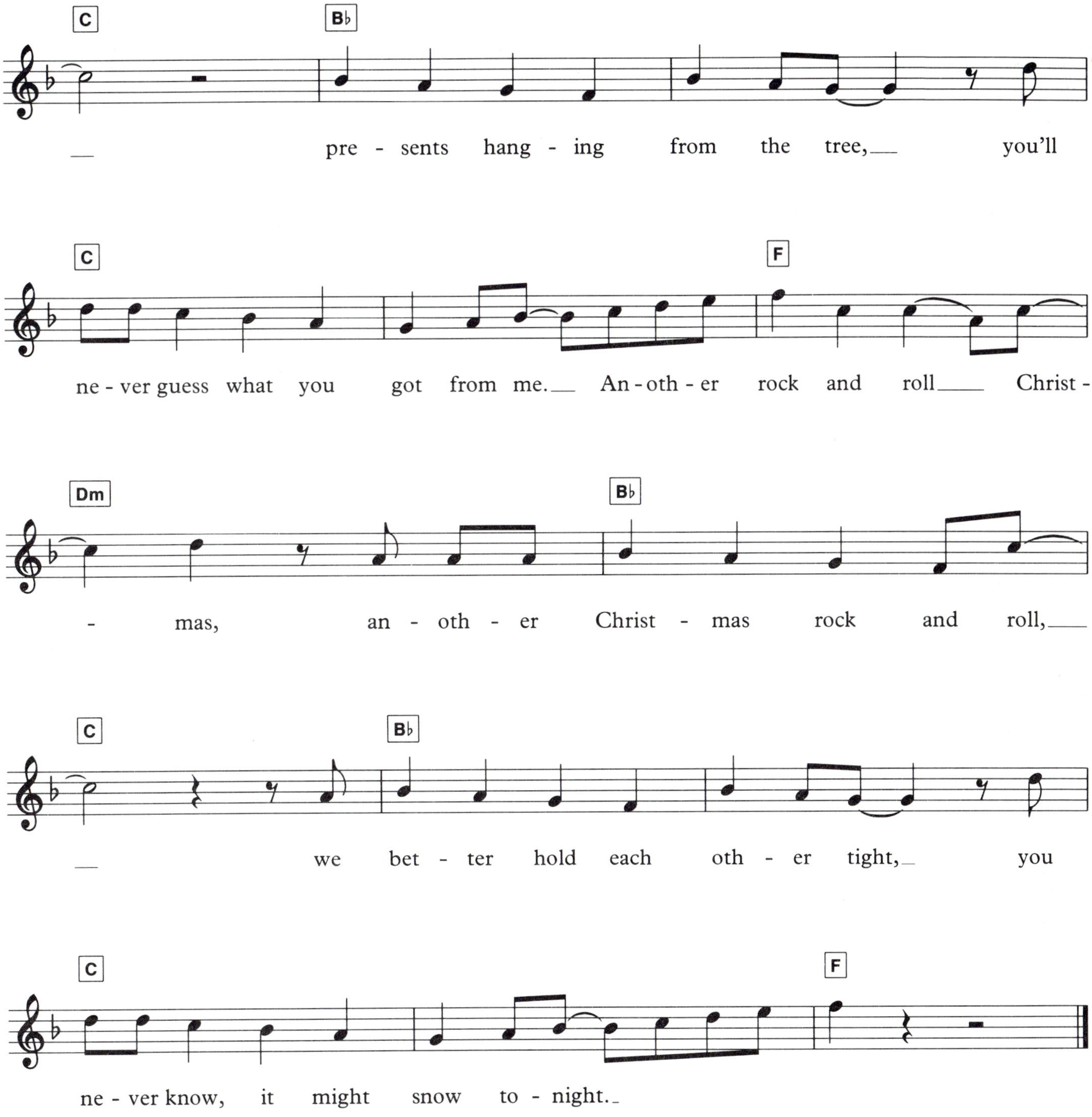

C Bb
pre - sents hang - ing from the tree, you'll
C F
ne - ver guess what you got from me. An - oth - er rock and roll Christ -
Dm Bb
- mas, an - oth - er Christ - mas rock and roll,
C Bb
we bet - ter hold each oth - er tight, you
C F
ne - ver know, it might snow to - night.

Bb
C
Dm
F

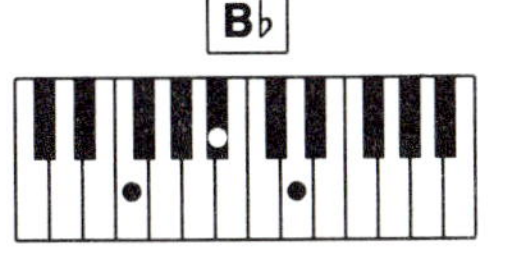

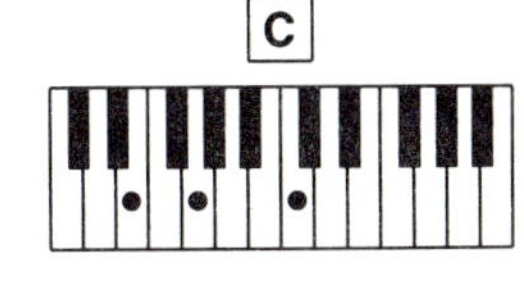

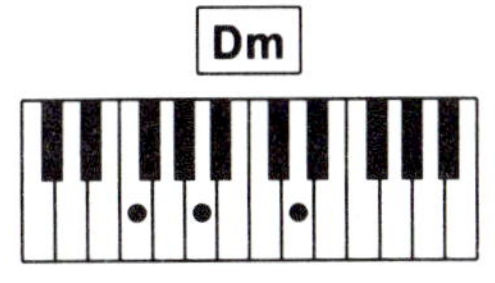

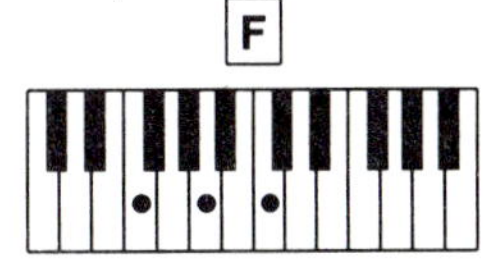

FROSTY THE SNOWMAN

Words & Music by Steve Nelson and Jack Rollins

Suggested Registration: Vibraphone
Rhythm: Swing
Tempo: ♩ = 166

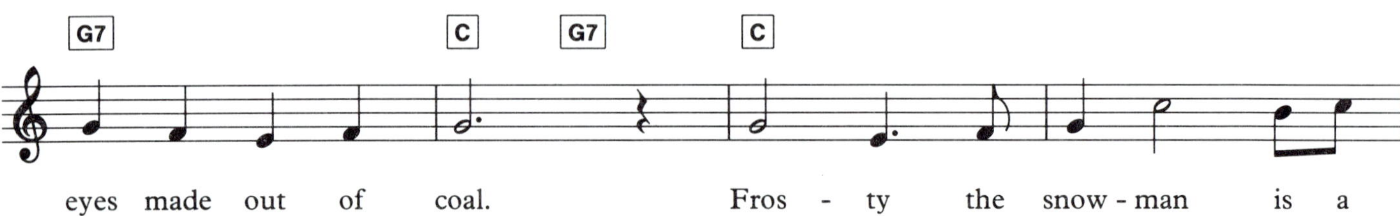

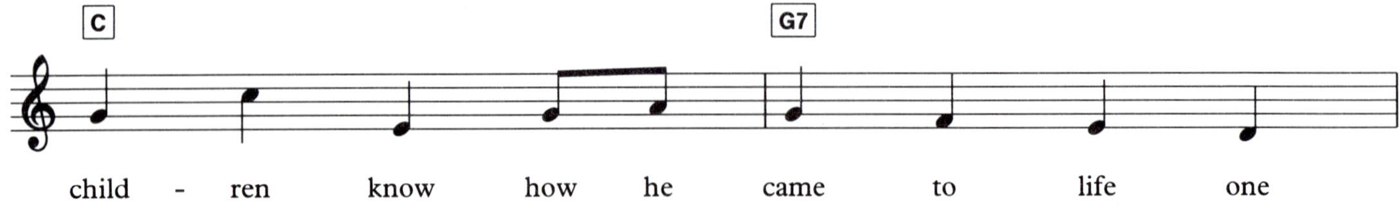

© 1950 & 1994 Chappell & Co Inc, USA
Carlin Music Corp, London NW1 8BD

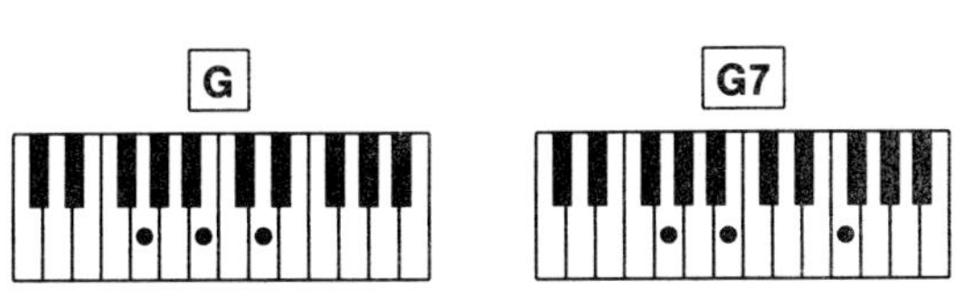

Dm G7 C G
old silk hat they found, for when they placed it
D7 G7
on his head, he be - gan to dance a - round. Oh,
C F
Fros - ty the snow - man was a - live as he could
C F
be, and the child - ren say he could
C G7 C
laugh and play just the same as you and me.
C D7 Dm Em F G G7

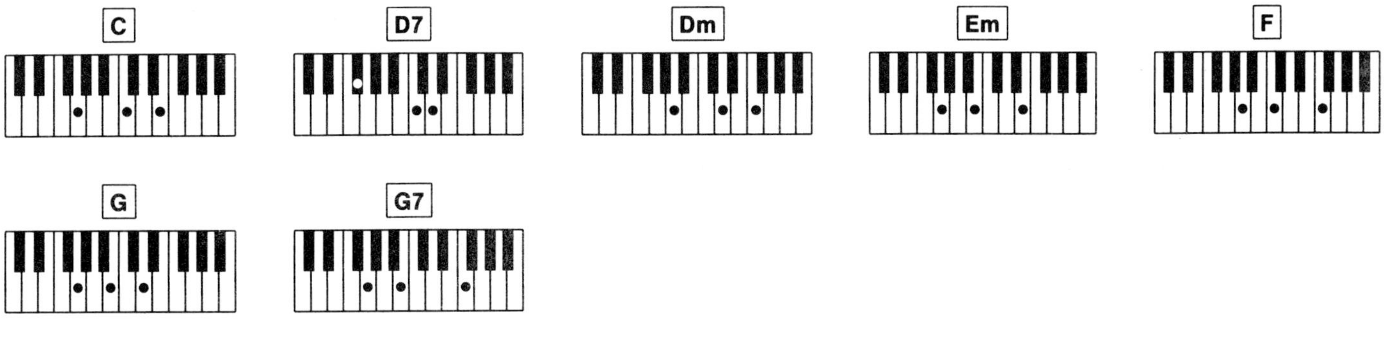

Have Yourself A Merry Little Christmas

Words & Music by Hugh Martin and Ralph Blane

Suggested Registration: Accordian
Rhythm: Slow Swing
Tempo: ♩ = 84

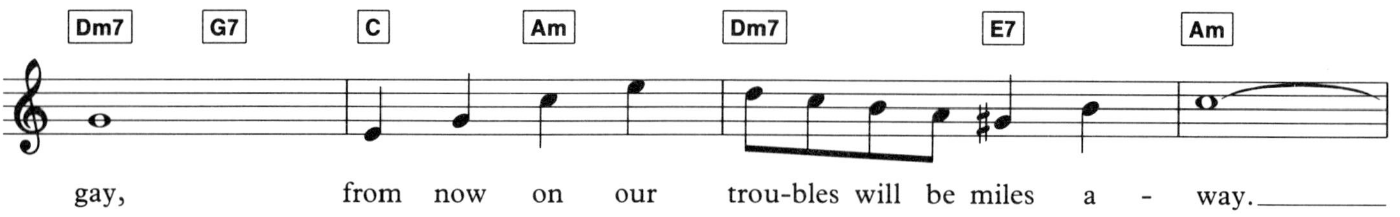

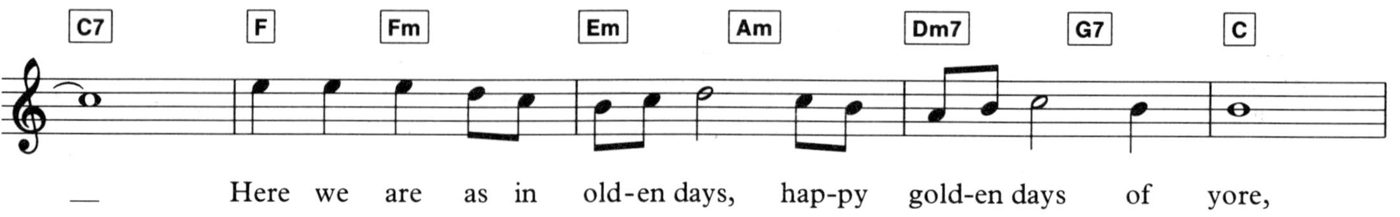

Am
B7
Em
D7
faith - ful friends who are dear to us, ga - ther near to us once

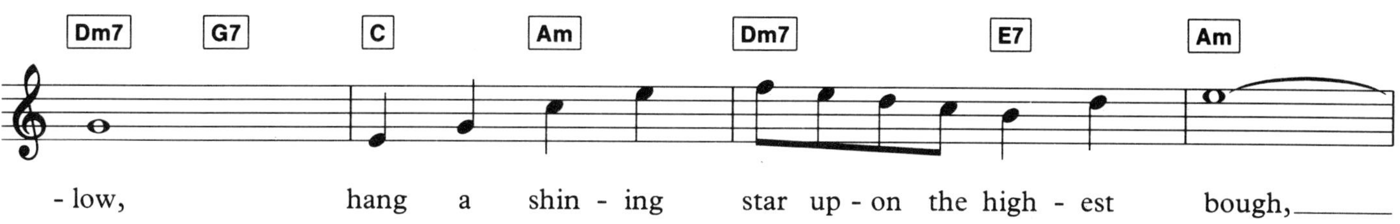
G7
C
Am
Dm7
G7
C
Am
more. Through the years we all will be to - ge - ther, if the fates al -

Dm7
G7
C
Am
Dm7
E7
Am
- low, hang a shin - ing star up - on the high - est bough,______

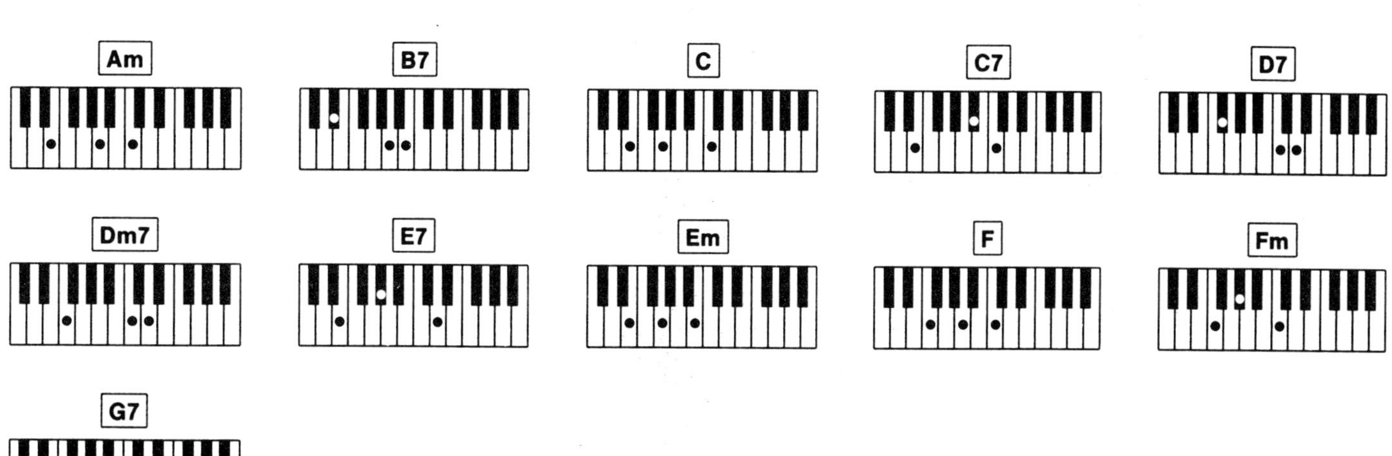
C7
F
Dm7
G7
C
F
C
__ and have your-self a mer-ry lit-tle Christ-mas now.____________
Am
B7
C
C7
D7
Dm7
E7
Em
F
Fm
G7

I Saw Mommy Kissing Santa Claus

Words & Music by Tommie Connor

Suggested Registration: Vibraphone
Rhythm: Swing
Tempo: ♩ = 150

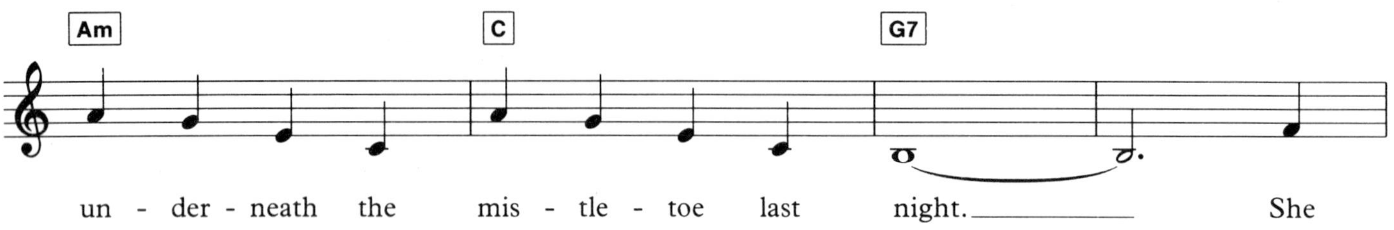

Em   Am   C7
San - ta Claus, un - der - neath his beard so sno - wy

F
white. _______ Oh what a laugh it would have

B7   C   Dm
been, if Dad - dy had on - ly seen Mom - my

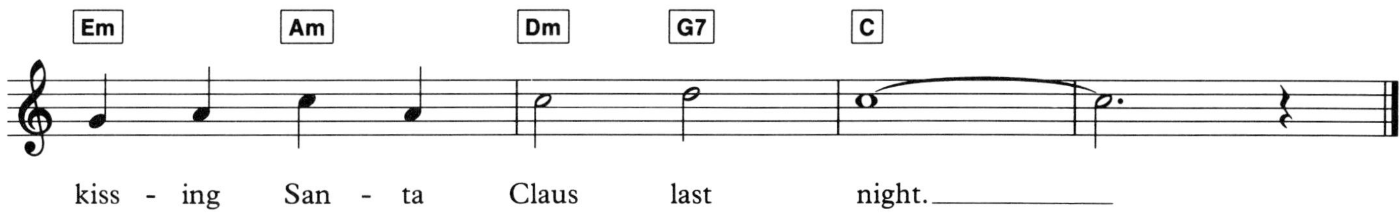

Em   Am   Dm   G7   C
kiss - ing San - ta Claus last night. _______

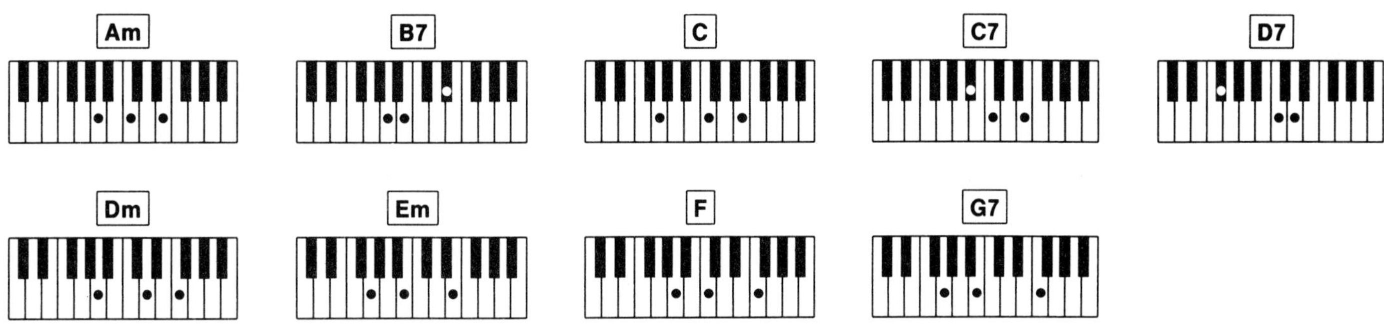

Am   B7   C   C7   D7
Dm   Em   F   G7

Jingle Bells

Traditional

Suggested Registration: Vibraphone
Rhythm: Dixie
Tempo: ♩ = 190

G
Jin - gle bells, jin - gle bells, jin - gle all the

C   G
way. Oh! What fun it is to ride in a

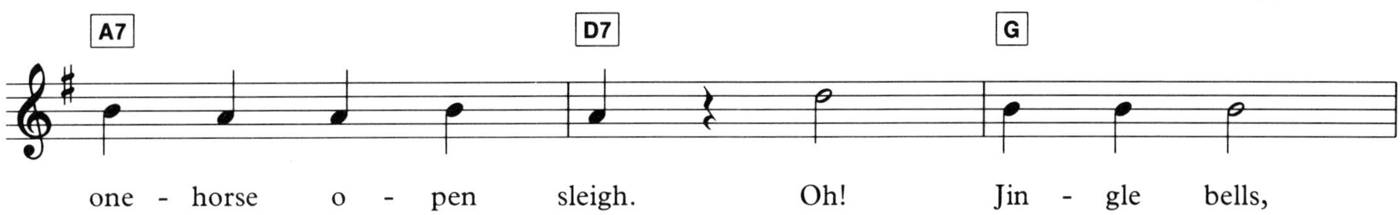

A7   D7   G
one - horse o - pen sleigh. Oh! Jin - gle bells,

C
jin - gle bells, jin - gle all the way. Oh! What fun it

G   D7   G
is to ride in a one - horse o - pen sleigh.

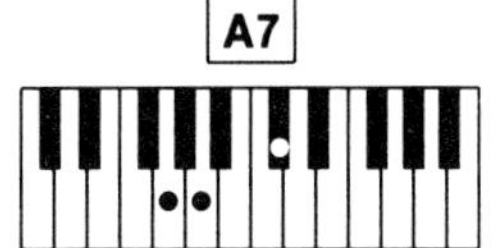

A7

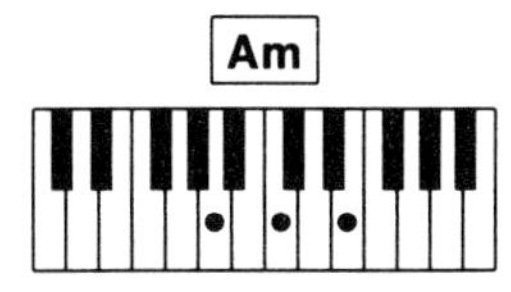

Am

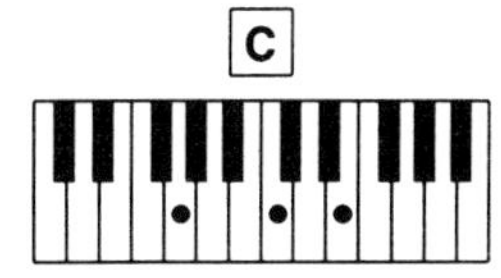

C

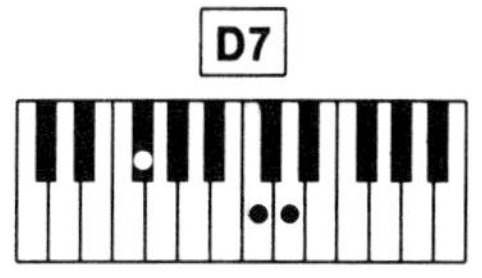

D7

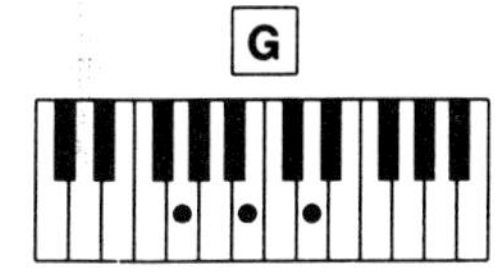

G

LAST CHRISTMAS

Words & Music by George Michael

Suggested Registration: Piano
Rhythm: Soft Rock
Tempo: ♩ = 94

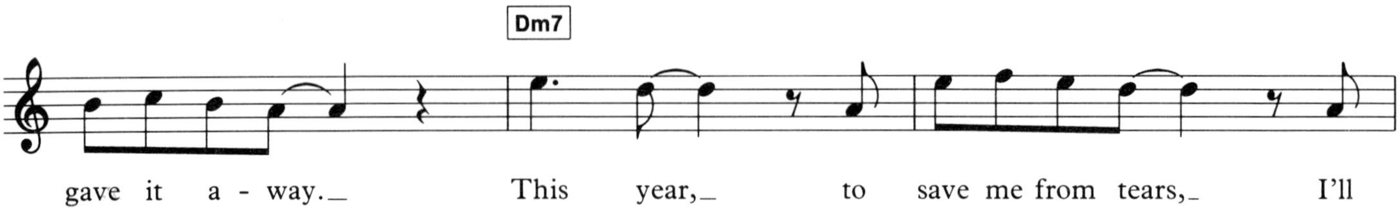

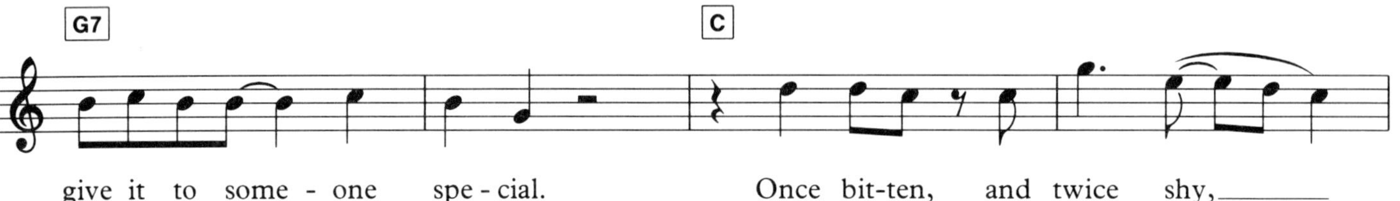

Dm7
__ love you', I meant it. Now__ I know what a fool________ I've been, but if you
G7
kissed me now,_ I know you'd fool me a - gain._
C
Last Christ - mas I
Am
gave you my heart, but the ve - ry next day you gave it a - way._
Dm7
This year,_ to save me from tears,_
G7
I'll give it to some - one
C
spe - cial.

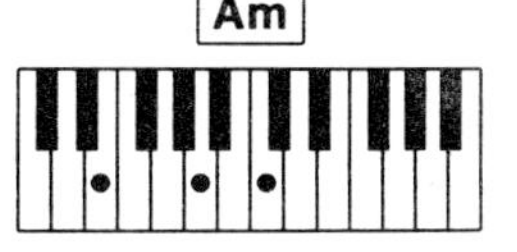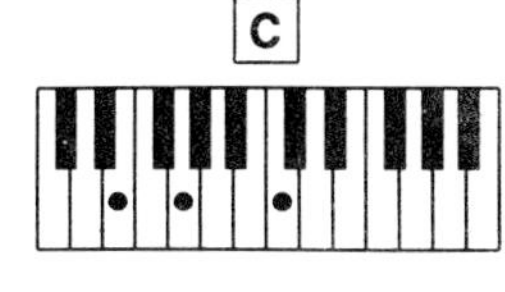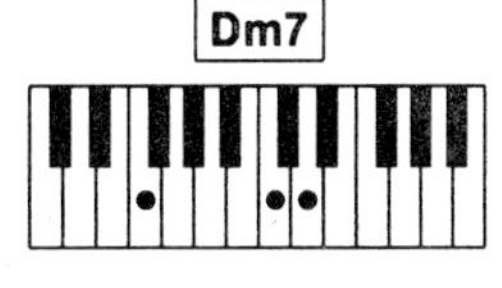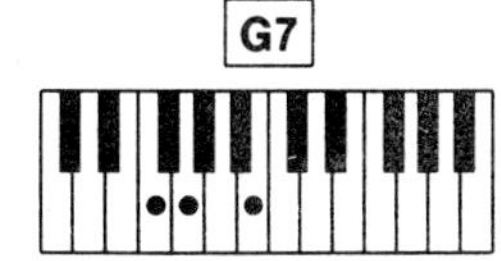

Am
C
Dm7
G7

Let It Snow! Let It Snow! Let It Snow!

Words by Sammy Cahn / Music by Jule Styne

Suggested Registration: Jazz Organ
Rhythm: Swing
Tempo: ♩ = 130

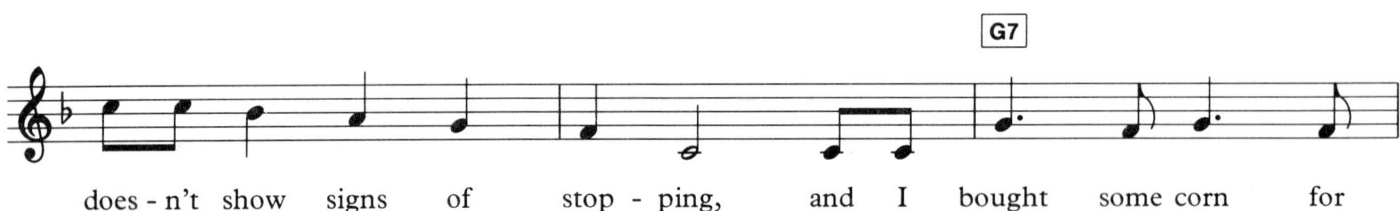

G7   C
- night,   how I'll hate   go - ing out   in the storm,   but if

D7   G7
you   real - ly hold   me   tight,   all the way home   I'll be

C   C7   F
warm.   The   fire   is   slow - ly   dy - ing,   and my

G7   C7   Bb   D7
dear,   we're still good - bye - ing,   but as long as you love me

Gm   C7   F
so,   Let it snow! Let it snow! Let it snow!

Bb   C   C7   D7   F

G7   Gm

THE LITTLE BOY THAT SANTA CLAUS FORGOT

Words & Music by Michael Carr, Tommie Connor and Jimmy Leach

Suggested Registration: Electric Piano
Rhythm: Swing
Tempo: ♩ = 80

© 1937 & 1994 Peter Maurice Music Co Ltd, London WC2H 0EA

G7   C7   F   Dm
- got,___ and good-ness knows he did-n't want a lot.___ He sent a note to San-ta for some
Gm   C7   Gm   C7
sol - diers and a drum, it broke his lit - tle heart when he found
Gm   C7   F   D7   G7
San - ta had - n't come. In the street he en - vies all those luc - ky boys,___ then
C7   Dm   B♭   B♭m
wan - ders home to last year's bro - ken toys. I'm so sor - ry for that lad-die, he
F   D7   Gm   C7   F
has - n't got a dad - dy, the lit - tle boy that San - ta Claus for - got.
B♭   B♭m   C7   D7   Dm
F   G7   Gm

LITTLE DONKEY

Words & Music by Eric Boswell

Suggested Registration: Flute
Rhythm: Soft Rock
Tempo: ♩ = 88

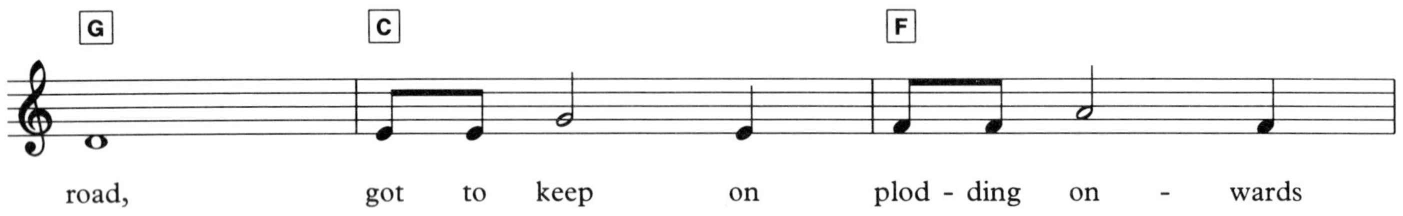

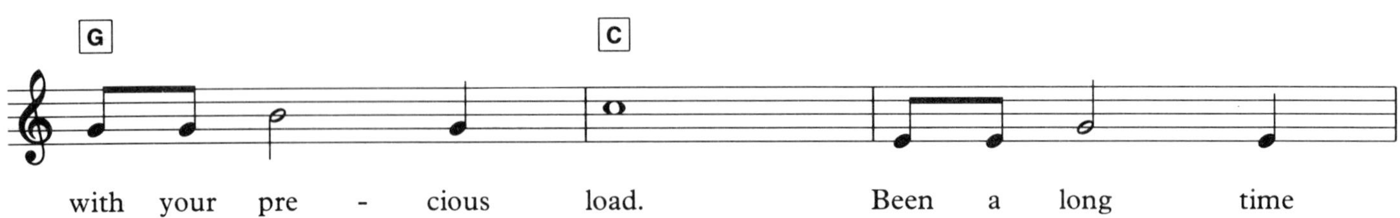

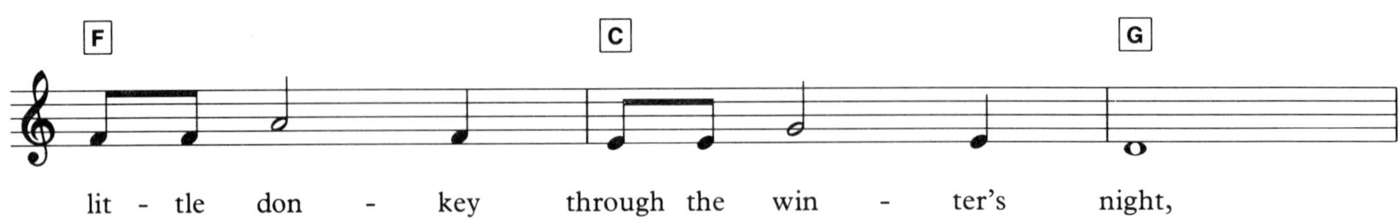

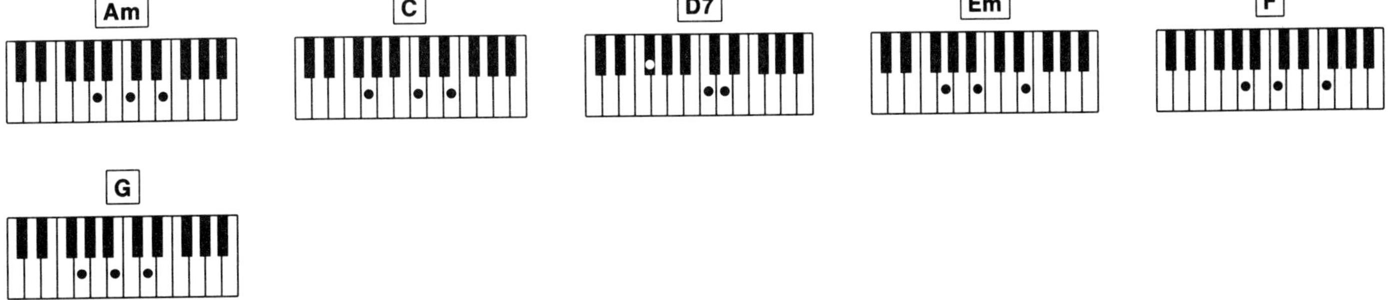

sight. Ring out those bells to - night,
Beth - le - hem, Beth - le - hem. Fol - low that
star to - night, Beth - le - hem, Beth - le - hem.
Lit - tle don - key, lit - tle don - key had a hea - vy day,
lit - tle don - key car - ry Ma - ry safe - ly on her way.
C Am Em
D7 G D7 G Am
Em D7 G D7 G
C F C G
C F G C
Am C D7 Em F
G

Little Drummer Boy

Words & Music by Harry Simeone, Henry Onorati and Katherine K Davis

Suggested Registration: Horn
Rhythm: Tango
Tempo: ♩ = 120

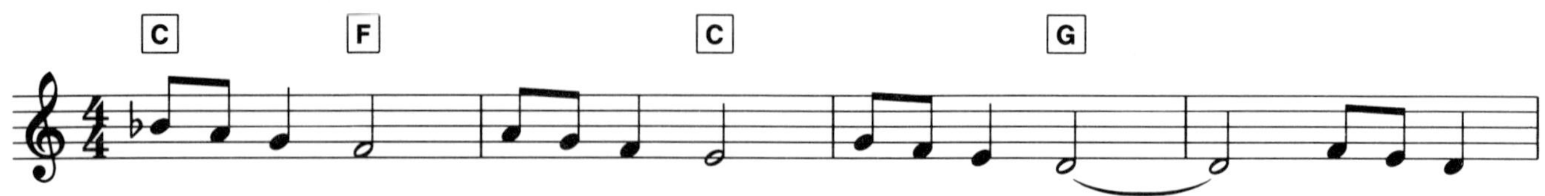

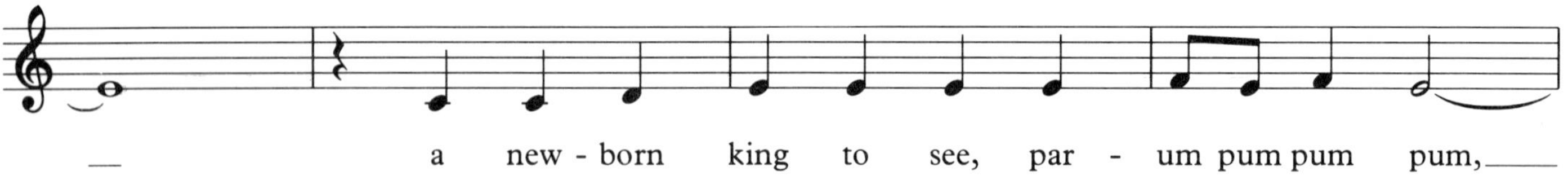

C
F
C
- fore the king, par - um pum pum pum, rum pum pum pum,
G
C
rum pum pum pum, so to
G
C
hon - our him, par - um pum pum pum, when we come.
F
C
G
C
C
F
G

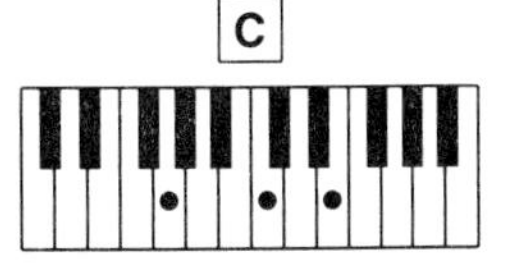

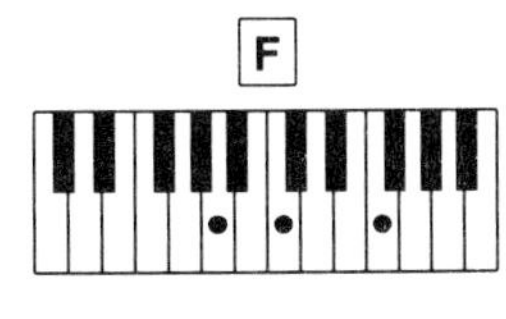

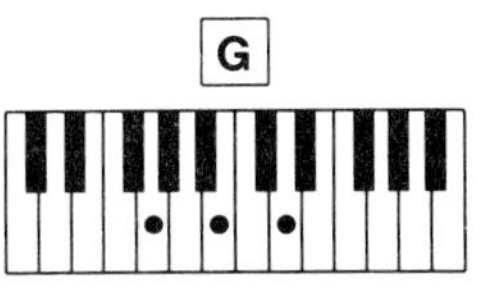

Mary's Boy Child

Words & Music by Jester Hairston

Suggested Registration: Marimba
Rhythm: Soft Rock
Tempo: ♩ = 96

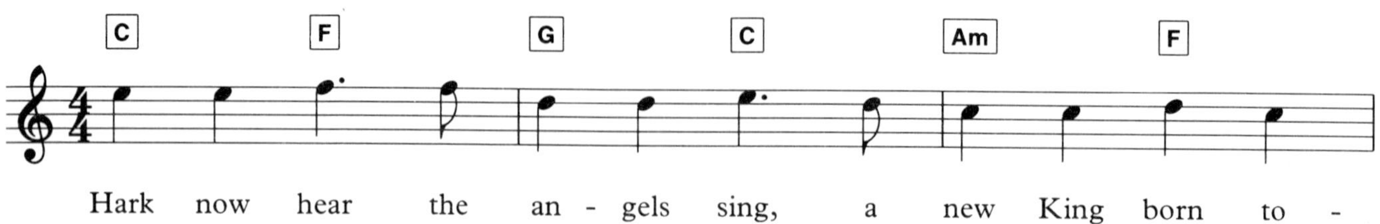

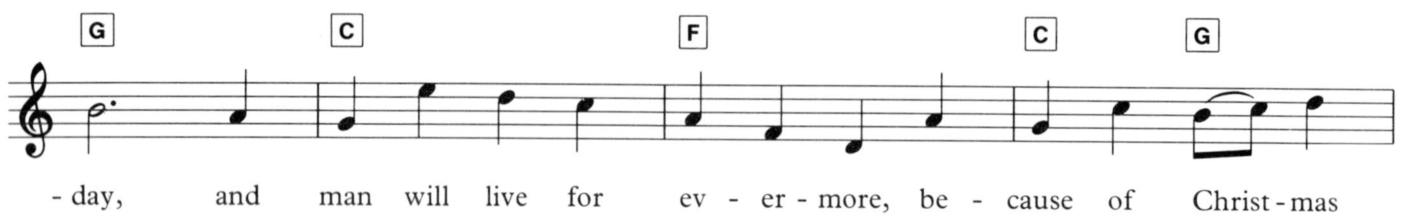

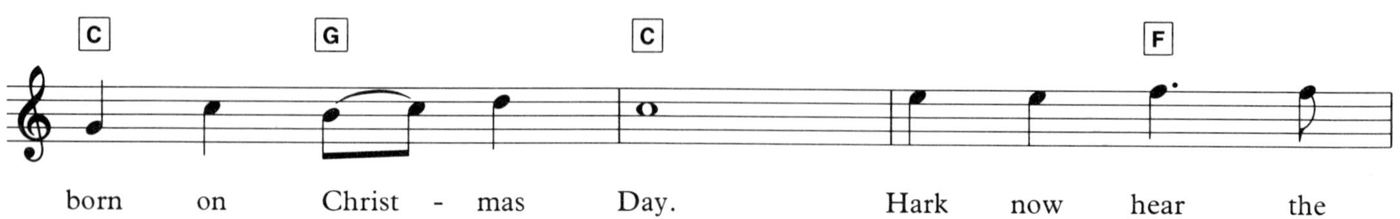

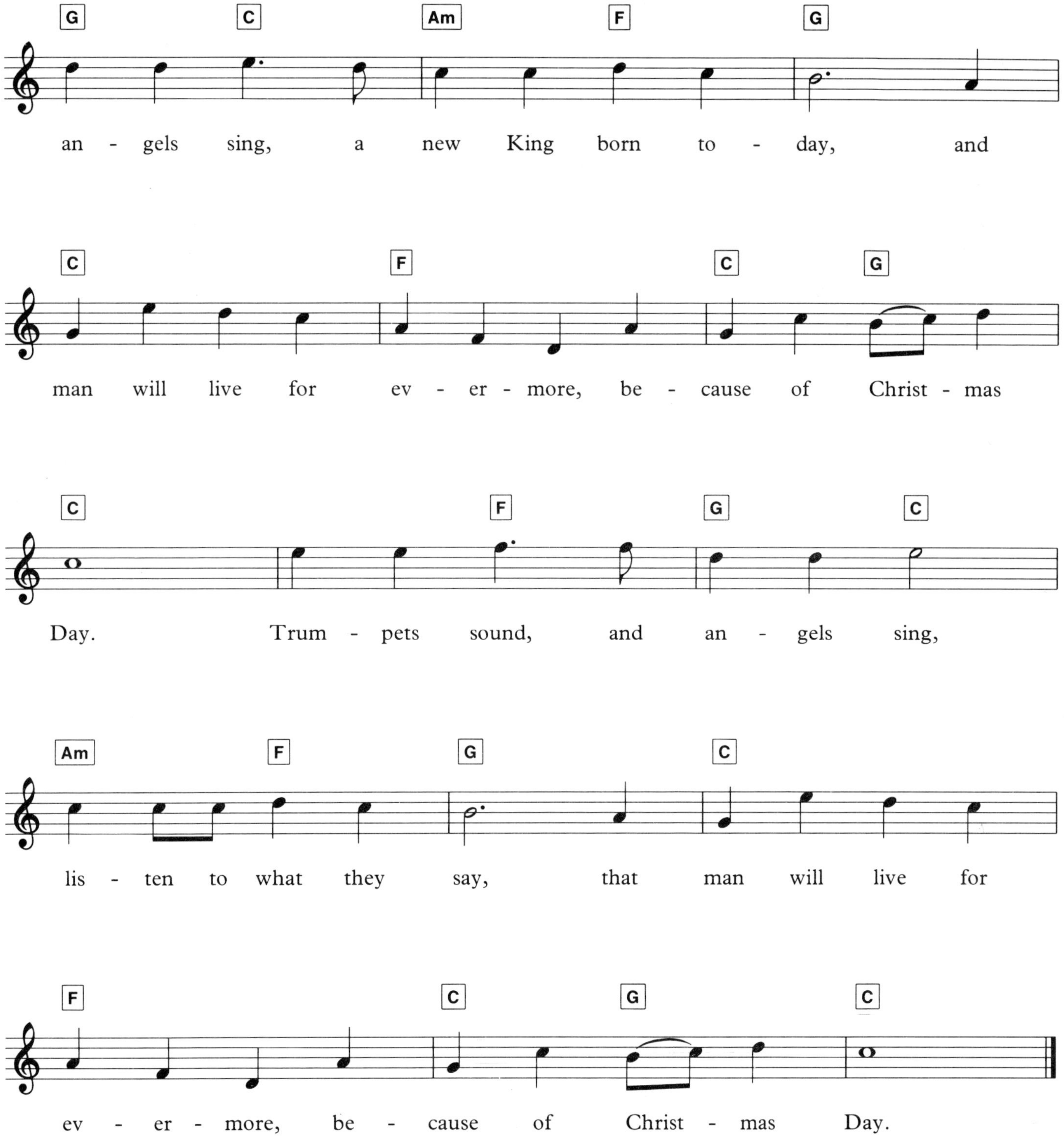

G C Am F G
an - gels sing, a new King born to - day, and
C F C G
man will live for ev - er - more, be - cause of Christ - mas
C F G C
Day. Trum - pets sound, and an - gels sing,
Am F G C
lis - ten to what they say, that man will live for
F C G C
ev - er - more, be - cause of Christ - mas Day.

Am
C
F
G

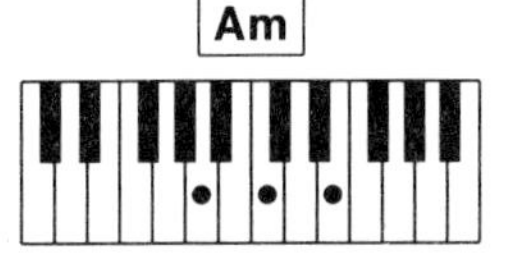

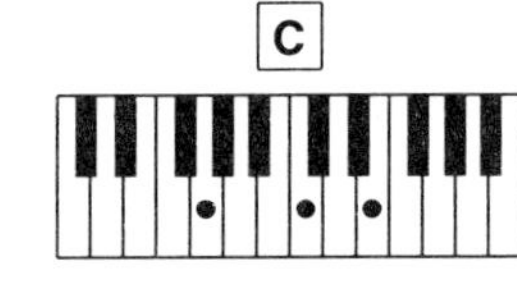

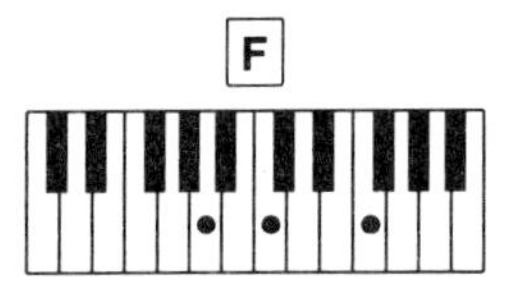

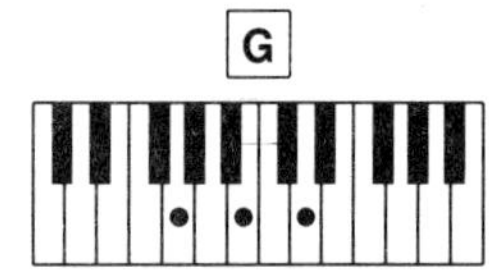

MERRY CHRISTMAS EVERYONE

Words & Music by Bob Heatlie

Suggested Registration: Saxophone
Rhythm: Pop Swing
Tempo: ♩ = 140

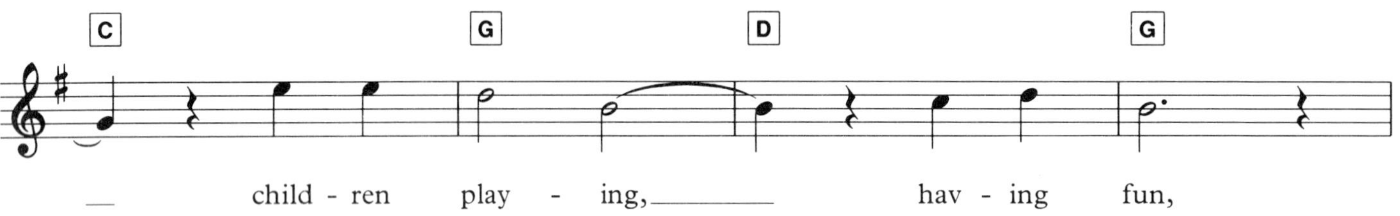

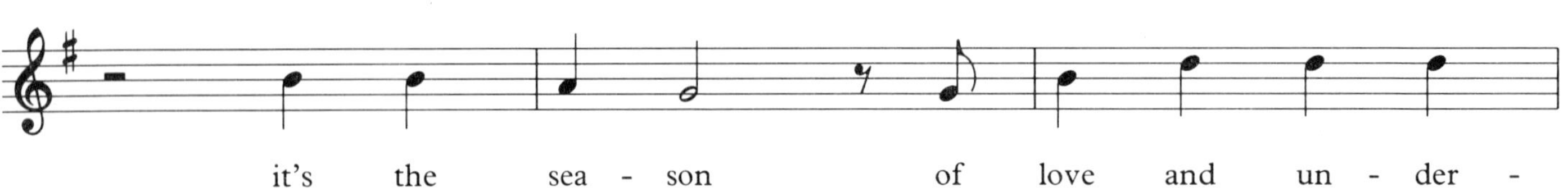

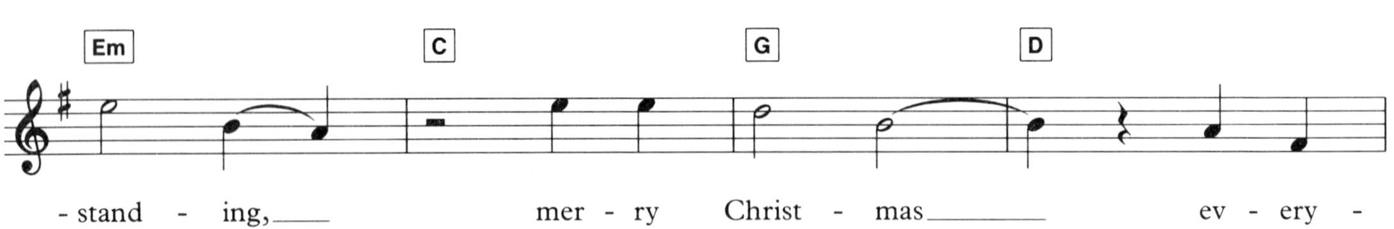

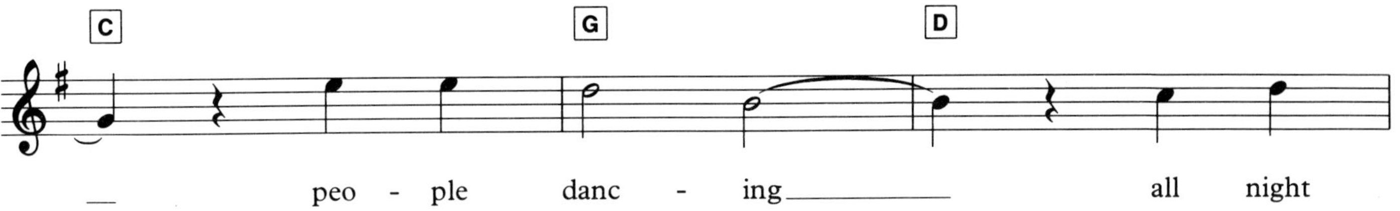
C
G
D
peo - ple danc - ing______ all night

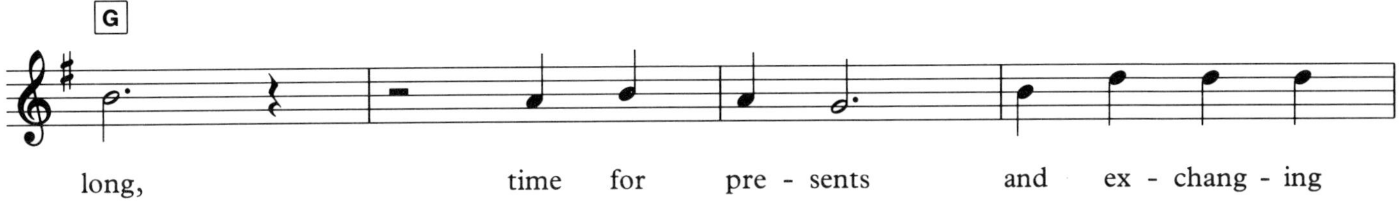
G
long, time for pre - sents and ex - chang - ing

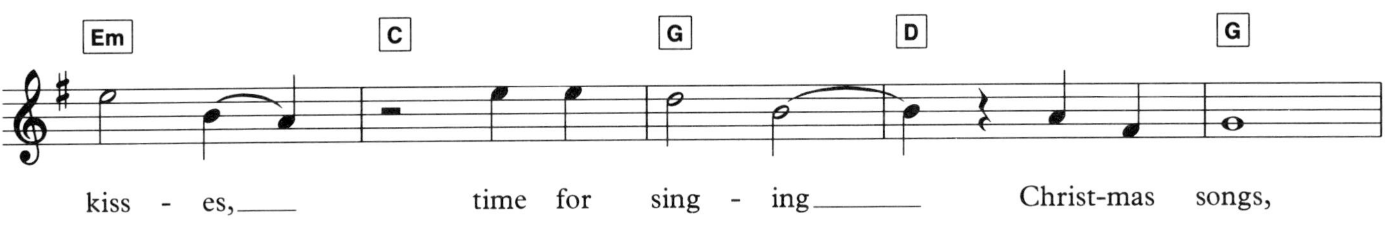
Em
C
G
D
G
kiss - es,____ time for sing - ing______ Christ-mas songs,

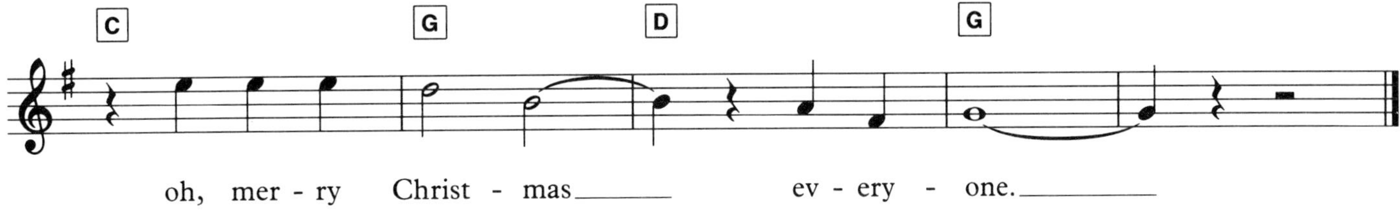
C
G
D
G
oh, mer - ry Christ - mas______ ev - ery - one.__________

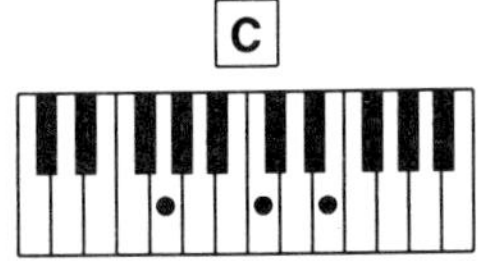
C

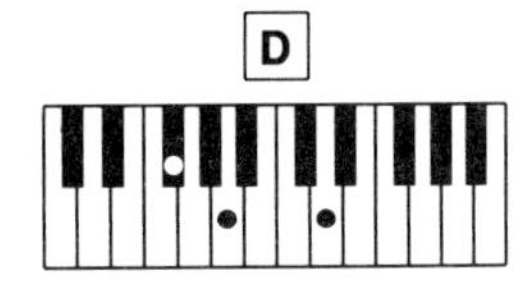
D

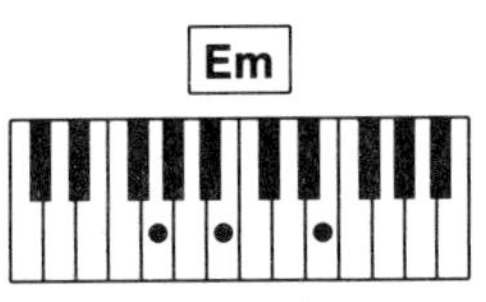
Em

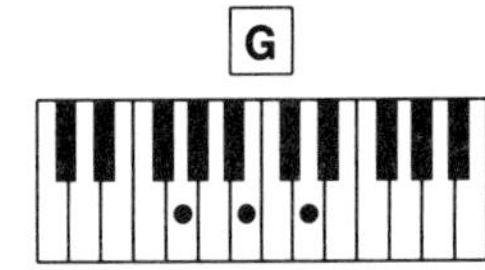
G

Mistletoe And Wine

Words by Leslie Stewart and Jeremy Paul / Music by Keith Strachan

Suggested Registration: Acoustic Guitar
Rhythm: Waltz
Tempo: ♩ = 132

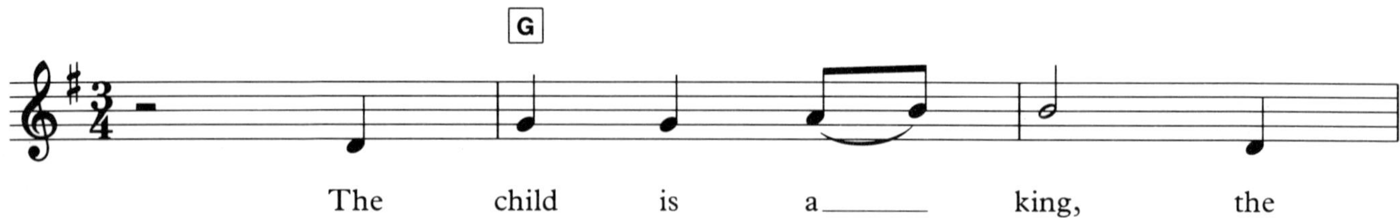

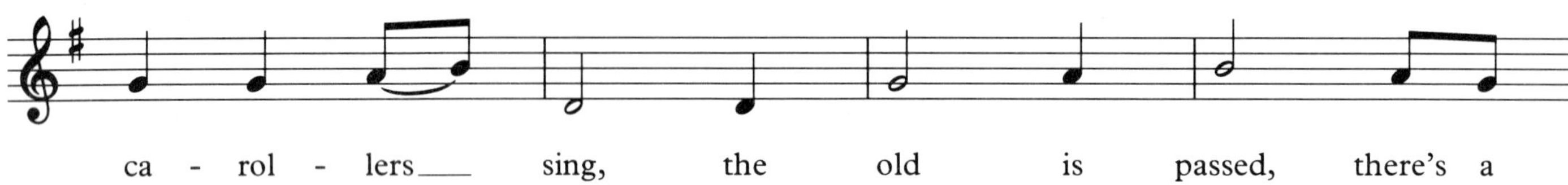

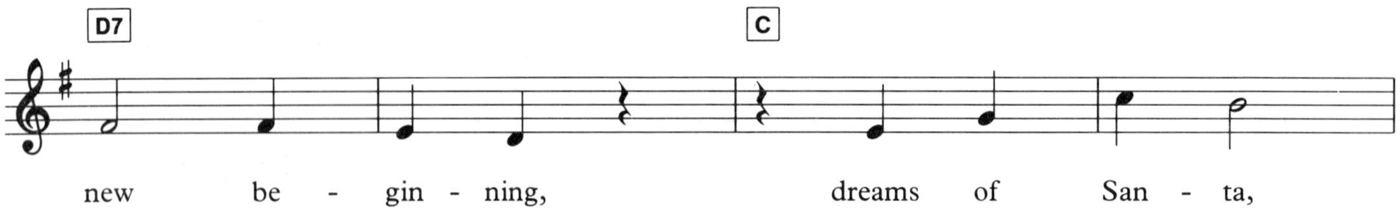

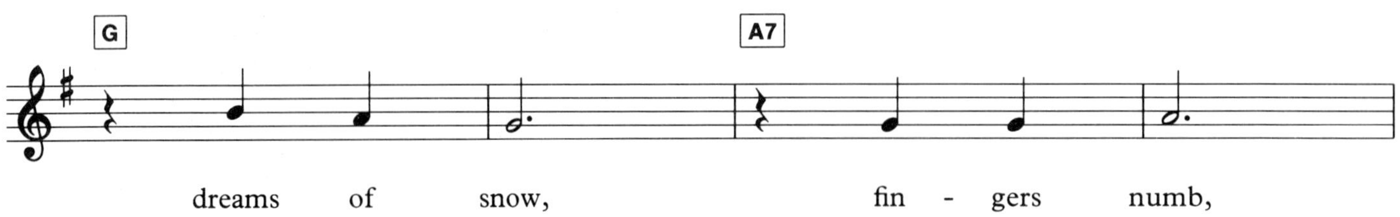

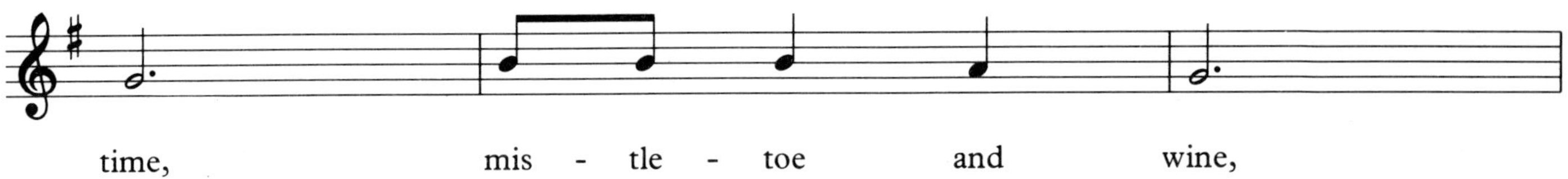

time,   mis - tle - toe   and   wine,

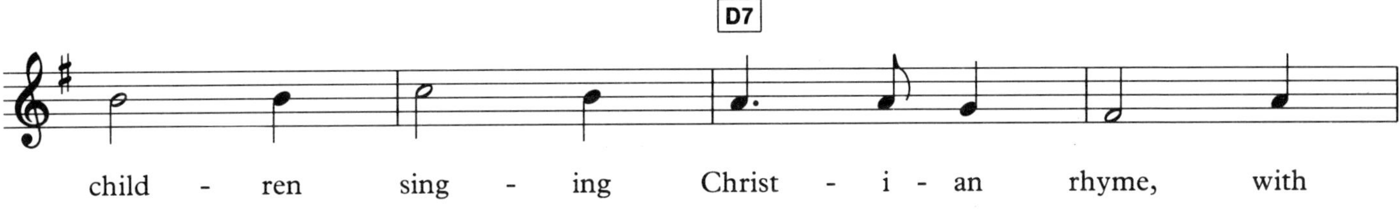

D7
child - ren sing - ing Christ - i - an rhyme,   with

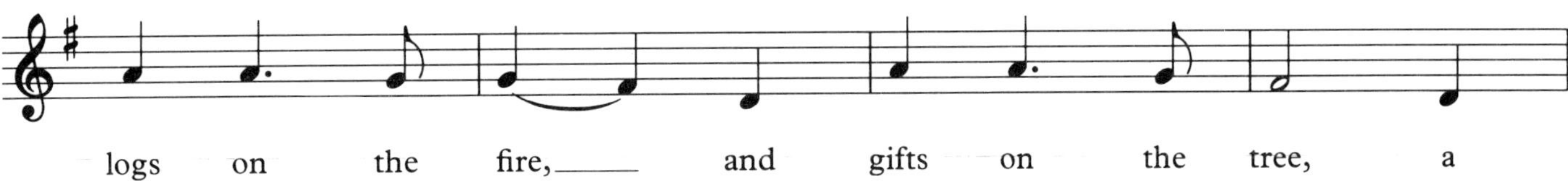

logs   on   the   fire,_____ and   gifts   on   the   tree,   a

G
time   to   re - joice   in   the   good   that   we   see.

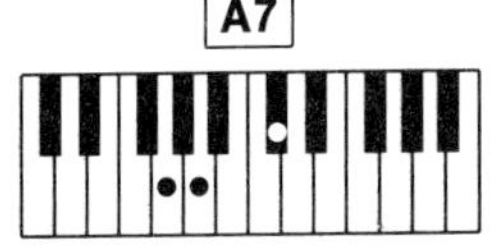

A7

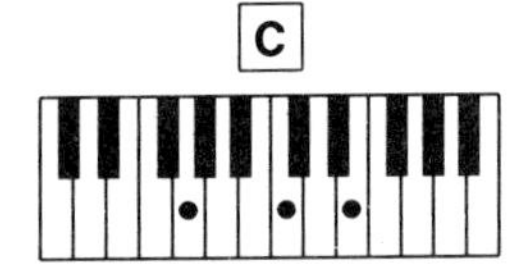

C

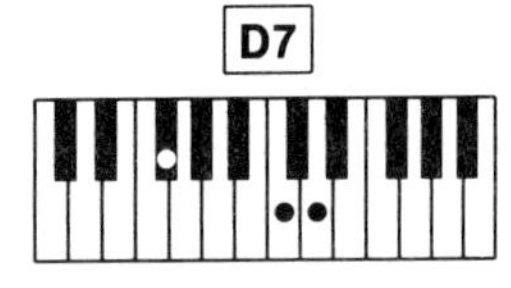

D7

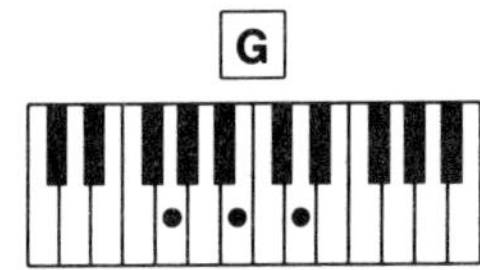

G

O Come All Ye Faithful

Traditional

Suggested Registration: French Horn
Rhythm: March
Tempo: ♩ = 100

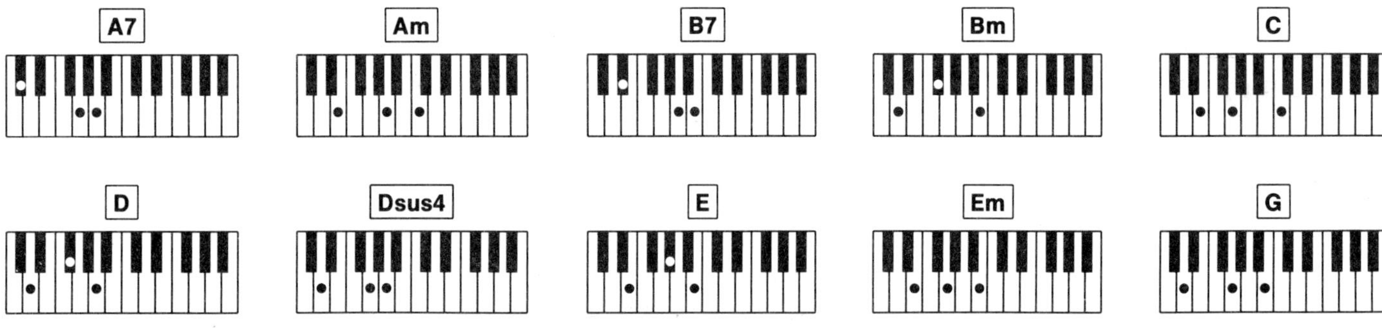

- dore him, O come let us a - dore him, O
Am C D Em Dsus4 D
come let us a - dore him Christ the
G
Lord. O come let us a - dore him, O
Am C
come let us a - dore him, O come let us a -
D Em Dsus4 D G
- dore him Christ the Lord.
A7 Am B7 Bm C
D Dsus4 E Em G

Rockin' Around The Christmas Tree

Words & Music by Johnny Marks

Suggested Registration: Tenor Saxophone
Rhythm: Pop Swing
Tempo: ♩ = 132

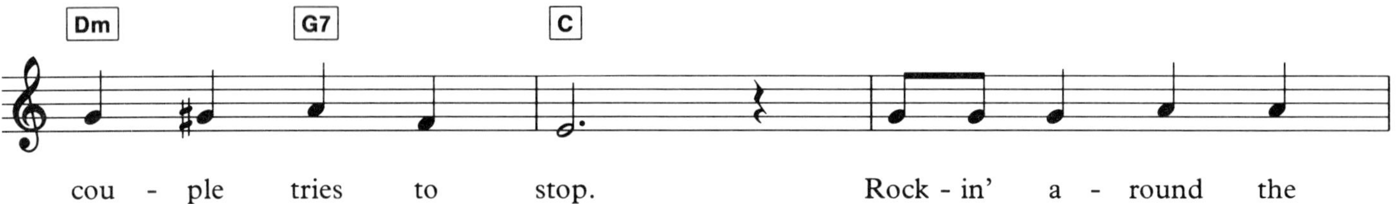

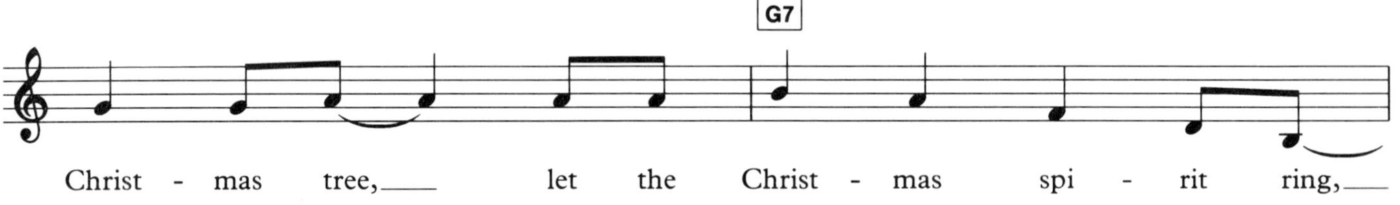

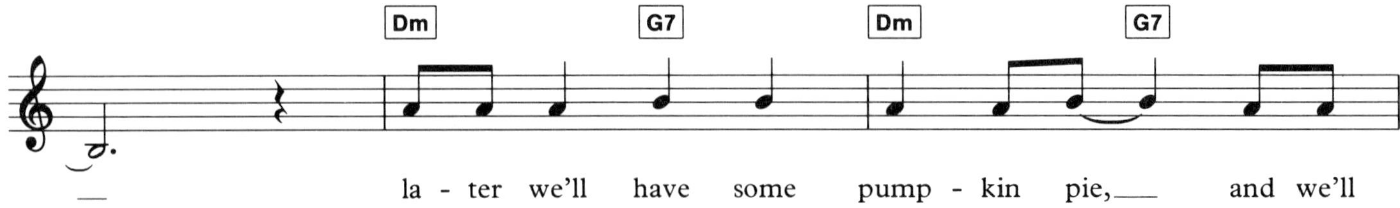

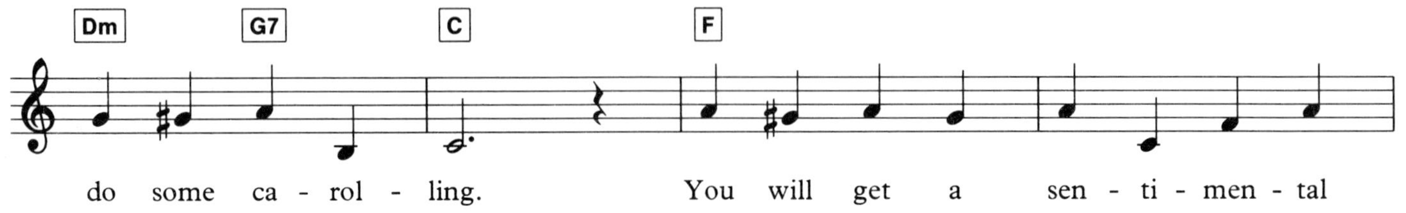

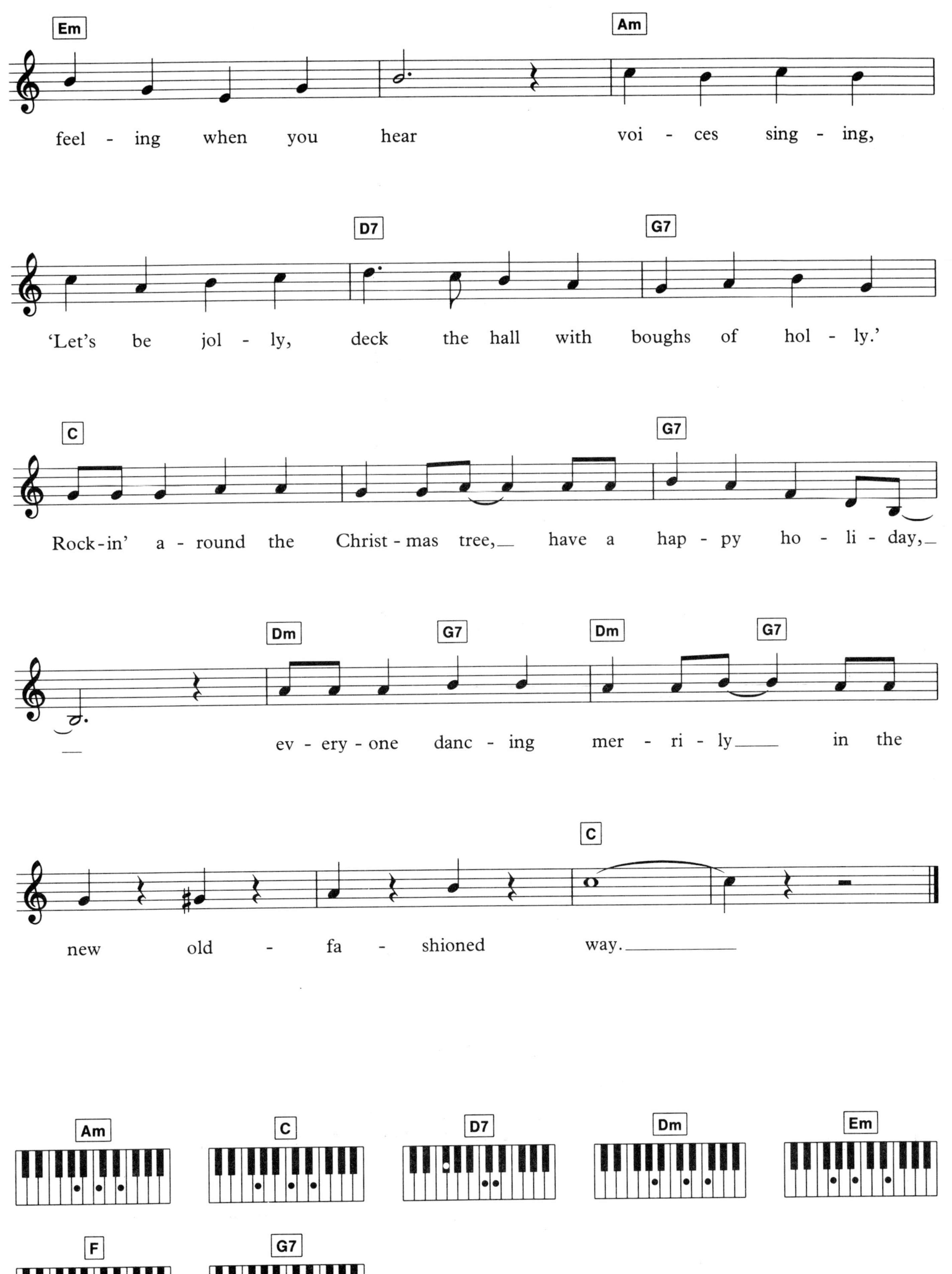

Em
Am
feel - ing when you hear voi - ces sing - ing,
D7
G7
'Let's be jol - ly, deck the hall with boughs of hol - ly.'
C
G7
Rock-in' a - round the Christ - mas tree,__ have a hap - py ho - li - day,__
Dm
G7
Dm
G7
ev - ery - one danc - ing mer - ri - ly__ in the
C
new old - fa - shioned way.__
Am
C
D7
Dm
Em
F
G7

Rudolph The Red-Nosed Reindeer

Words & Music by Johnny Marks

Suggested Registration: Clarinet
Rhythm: Swing
Tempo: ♩ = 132

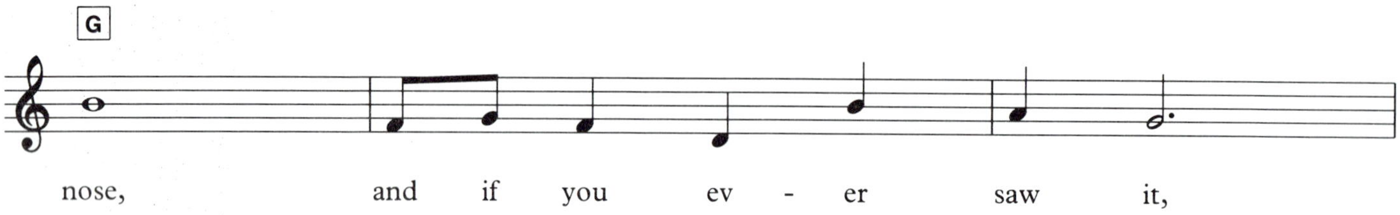

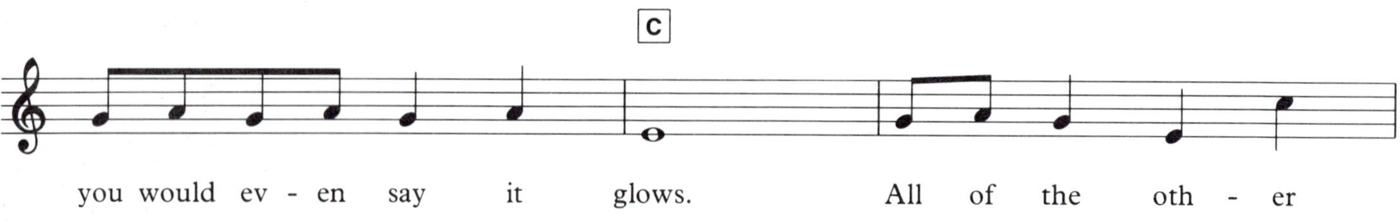

F   C   G   C
Then one fog - gy Christ - mas Eve, San - ta came to say,
G   Em   Am   D7
'Ru - dolph with your nose so bright, won't you guide my
G   C
sleigh to - night?' Then how the rein - deer loved him,
G
as they shout - ed out with glee, 'Ru - dolph the red - nosed
C
rein - deer, you'll go down in his - to - ry.'
Am   C   D7   Em   F
G

SANTA CLAUS IS COMIN' TO TOWN

Words by Haven Gillespie / Music by J Fred Coots

Suggested Registration: Synth Reed
Rhythm: Pop Swing
Tempo:  = 132

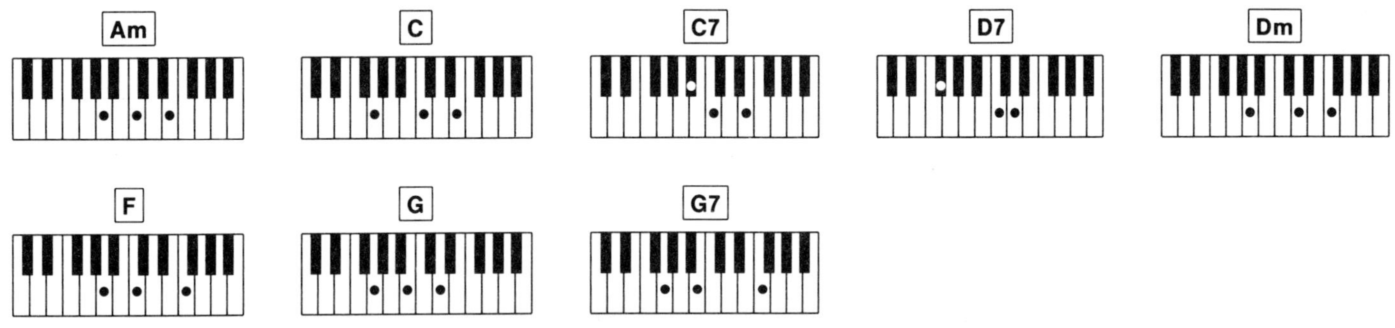

C7   F   D7
knows when you're a - wake, he knows if you've been

G   D7   G7
bad or good, so be good for good - ness sake. You

C   F
bet - ter watch out, you bet - ter not cry, you

C   F
bet - ter not pout, I'm tell - ing you why,

C   Am   Dm   G7   C   F   C
San - ta Claus is com - ing to town.

Am   C   C7   D7   Dm
F   G   G7

Silent Night

Traditional

Suggested Registration: Strings
Rhythm: Waltz
Tempo: ♩ = 96

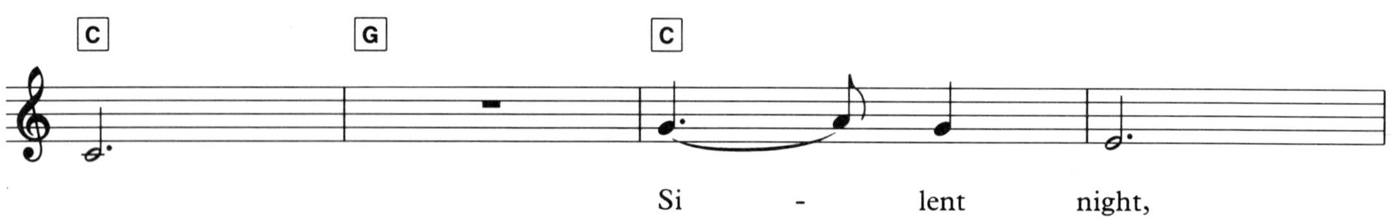

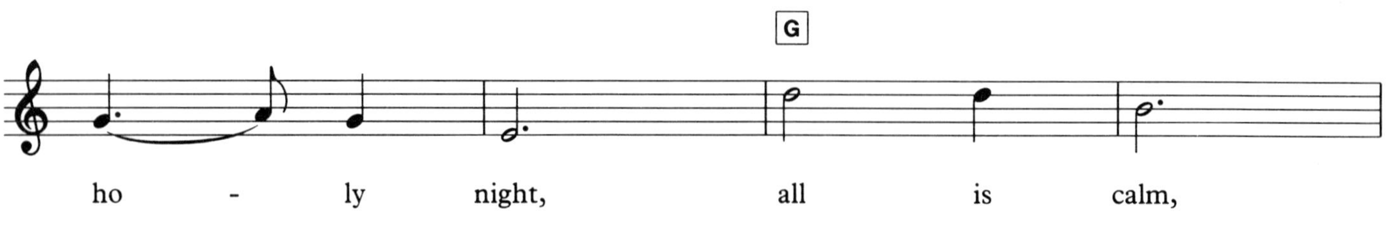

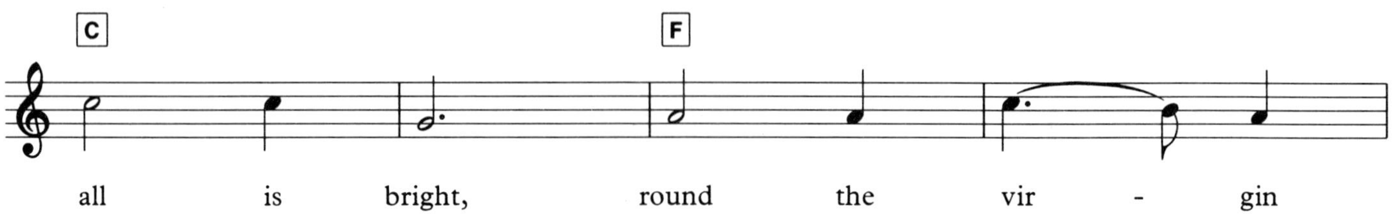

C
F
mo - ther and child, ho - ly

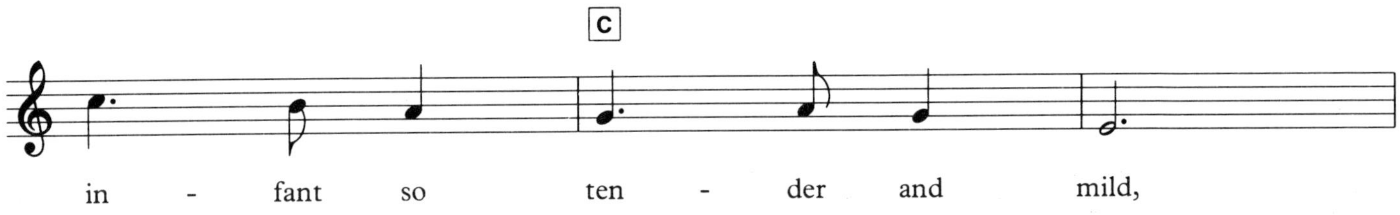
C
in - fant so ten - der and mild,

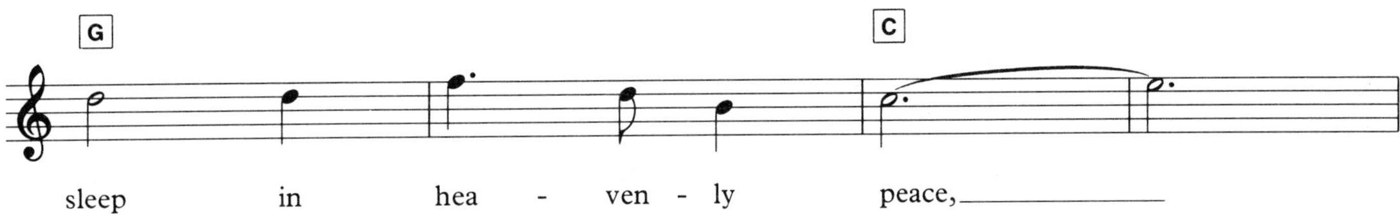
G
C
sleep in hea - ven - ly peace,______

G
C
sleep______ in hea - ven - ly peace.______

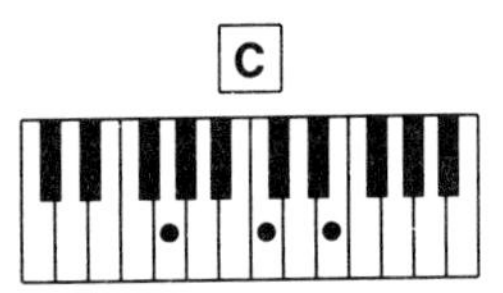
C

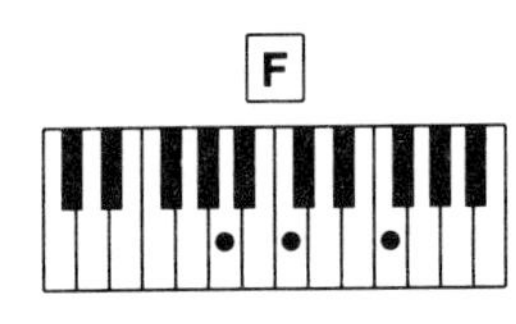
F

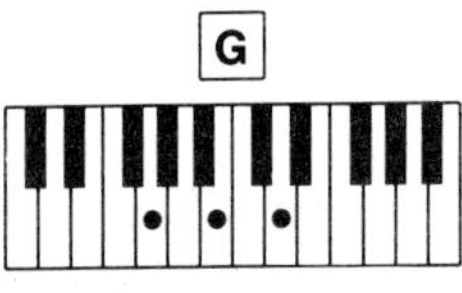
G

Silver Bells

Words & Music by Jay Livingston and Ray Evans

Suggested Registration: Celeste
Rhythm: Waltz
Tempo: ♩ = 112

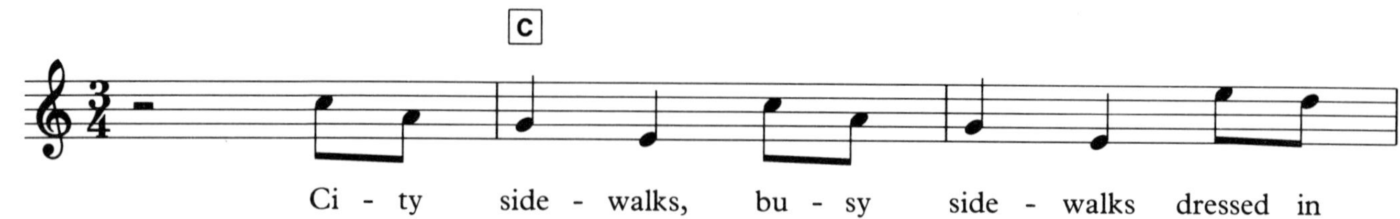

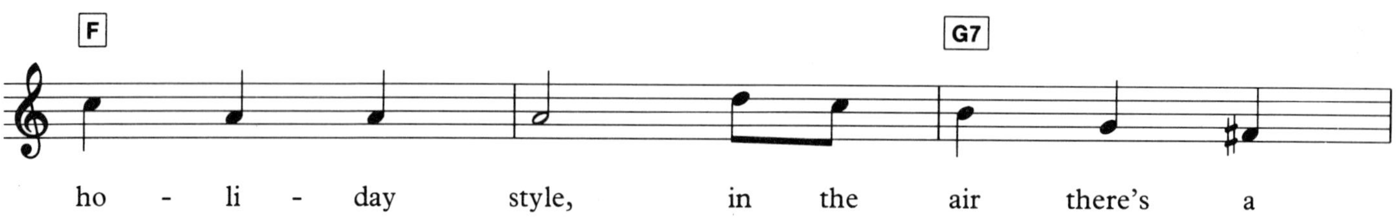

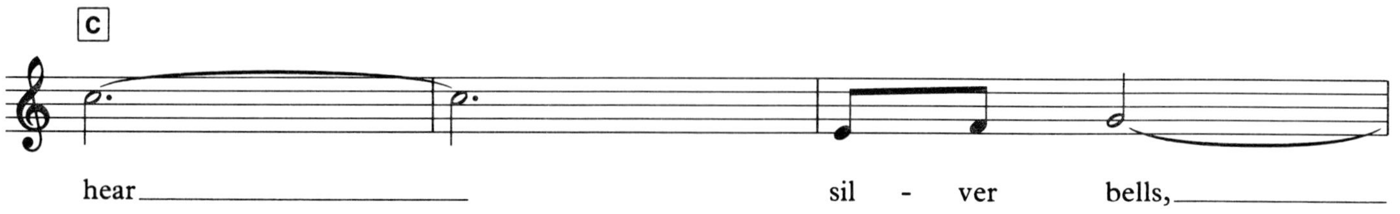

F
sil - ver bells.

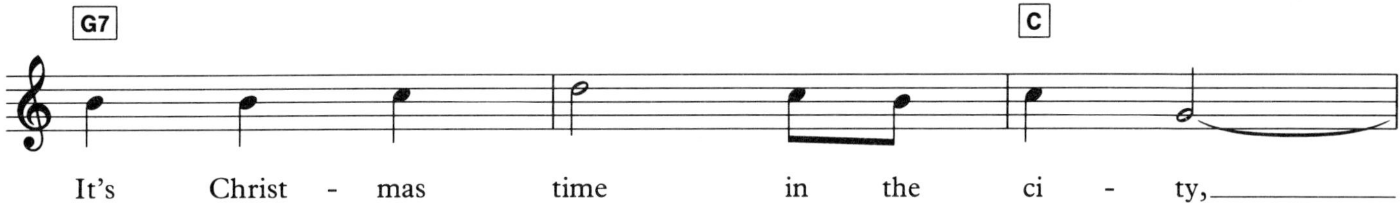
G7
C
It's Christ - mas time in the ci - ty,

ring - a - ling,

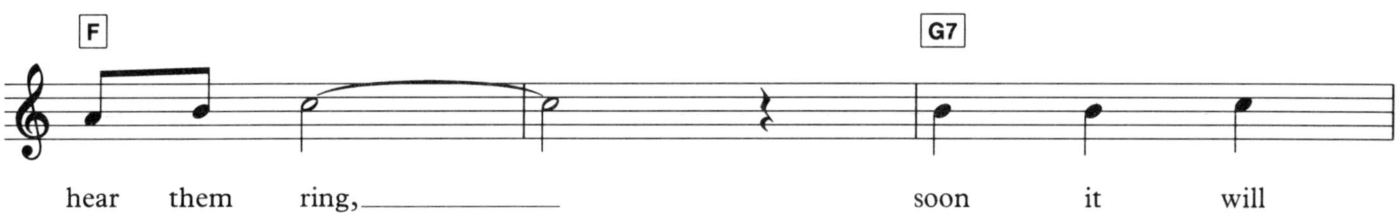
F
G7
hear them ring, soon it will

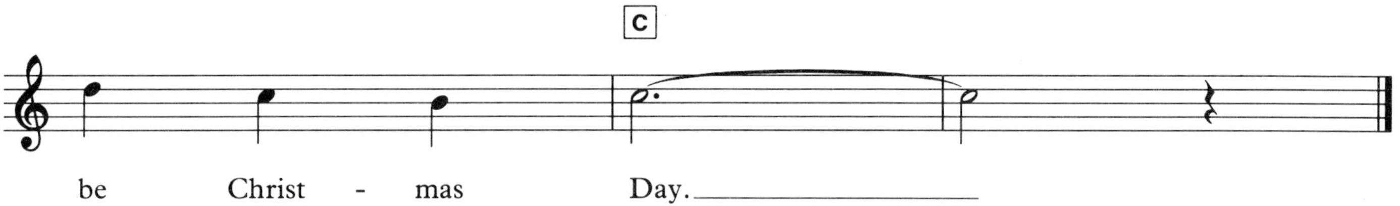
C
be Christ - mas Day.

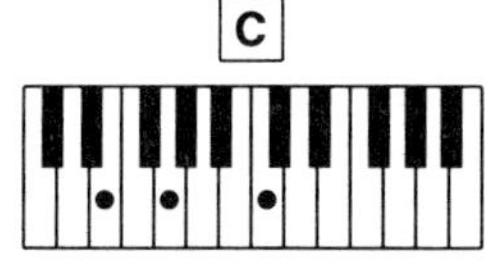
C

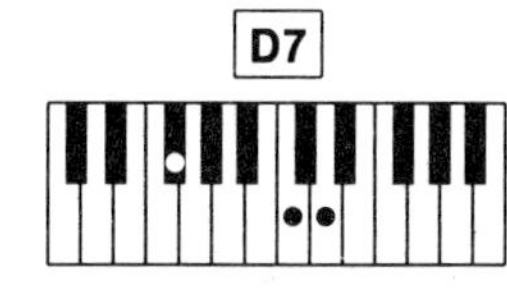
D7

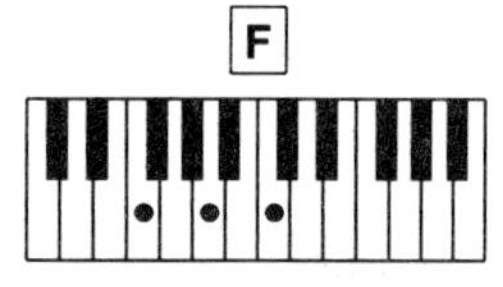
F

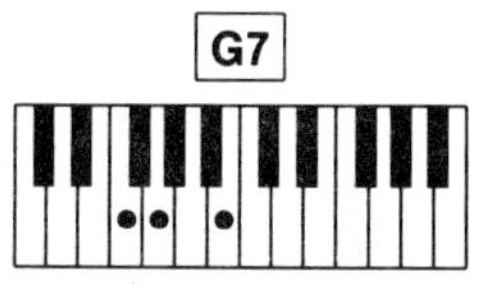
G7

We Wish You A Merry Christmas

Traditional

Suggested Registration: Harpsichord
Rhythm: Waltz
Tempo: ♩ = 112

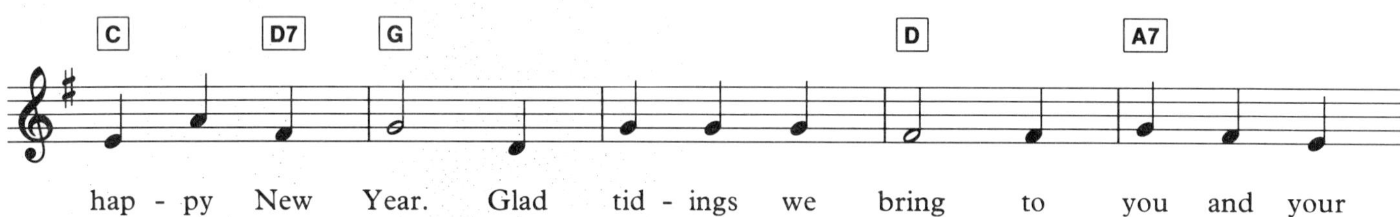

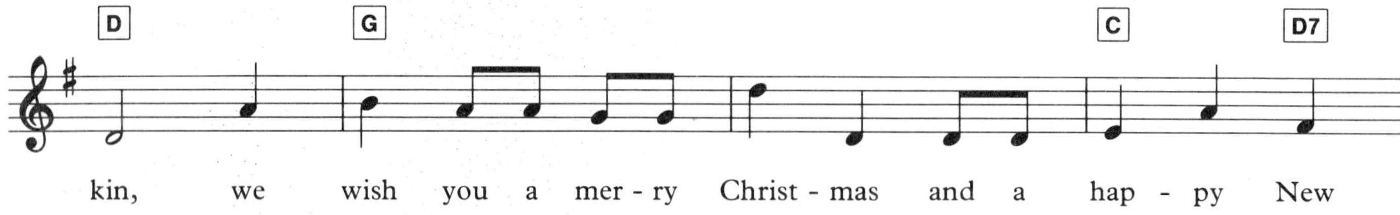

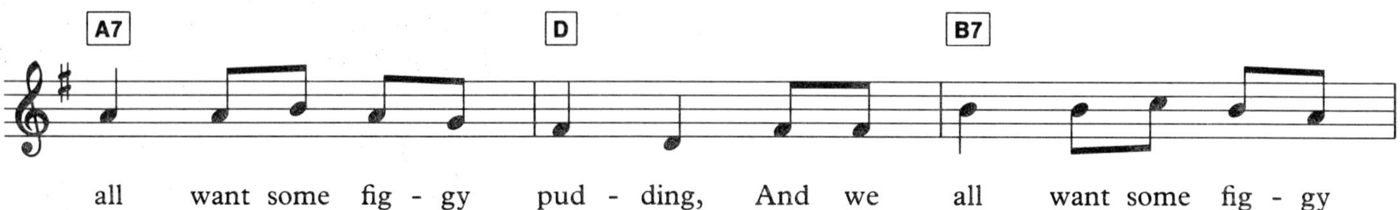

Em   C   D7   G
pud - ding,   so   bring   some   out   here.   And   we   won't   go   un - til   we've
C   A7   D
got   some,   and   we   won't   go   un - til   we've   got   some,   and   we
B7   Em   C   D7
won't   go   un - til   we've   got   some,   so   bring   some   out
G   D   A7   D
here.   Glad   tid - ings   we   bring   to   you   and   your   kin,   we
G   C   D7   G
wish   you   a   mer - ry   Christ - mas   and   a   hap - py   New   Year.
A7   B7   C   D   D7
Em   G

When A Child Is Born

Words by Fred Jay / Music by Zacar

Suggested Registration: Electric Piano
Rhythm: Soft Rock
Tempo: ♩ = 76

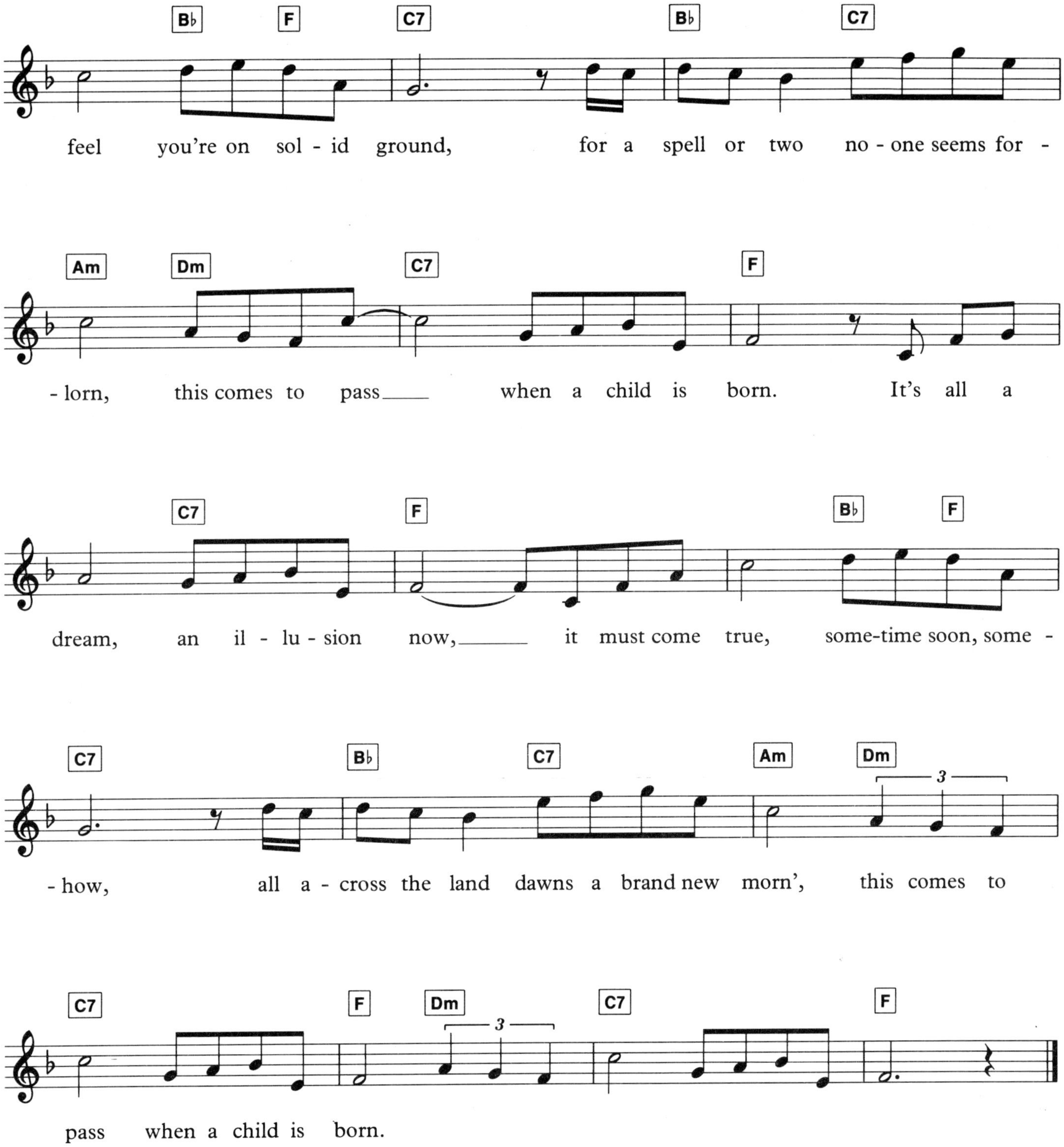

B♭ F C7 B♭ C7
feel you're on sol - id ground, for a spell or two no - one seems for -
Am Dm C7 F
- lorn, this comes to pass when a child is born. It's all a
C7 F B♭ F
dream, an il - lu - sion now, it must come true, some-time soon, some -
C7 B♭ C7 Am Dm
- how, all a - cross the land dawns a brand new morn', this comes to
C7 F Dm C7 F
pass when a child is born.

Am
B♭
C7
Dm
F

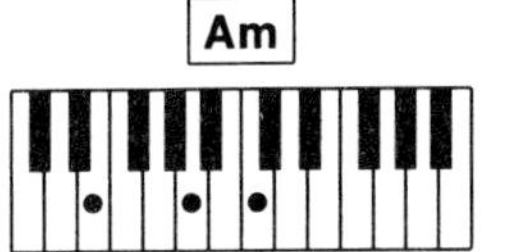

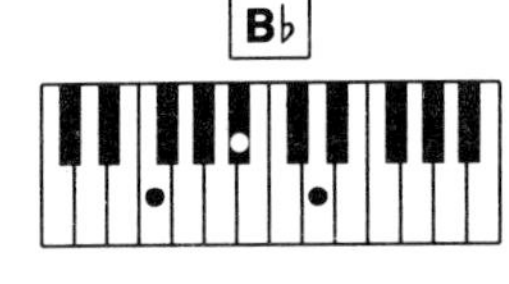

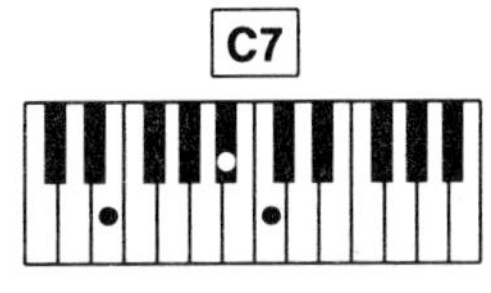

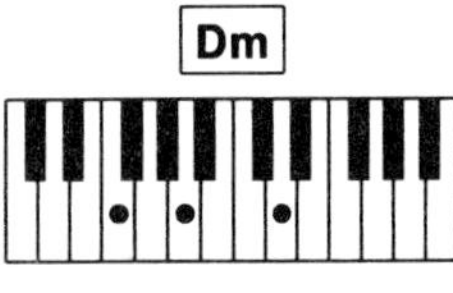

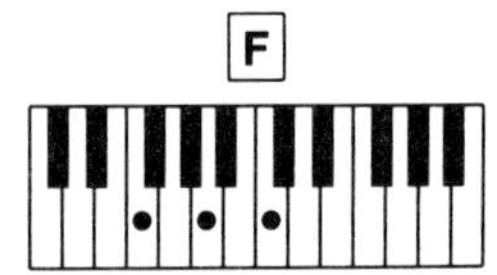

Winter Wonderland

Words by Dick Smith / Music by Felix Bernard

Suggested Registration: Vibraphone
Rhythm: Swing
Tempo: ♩ = 116

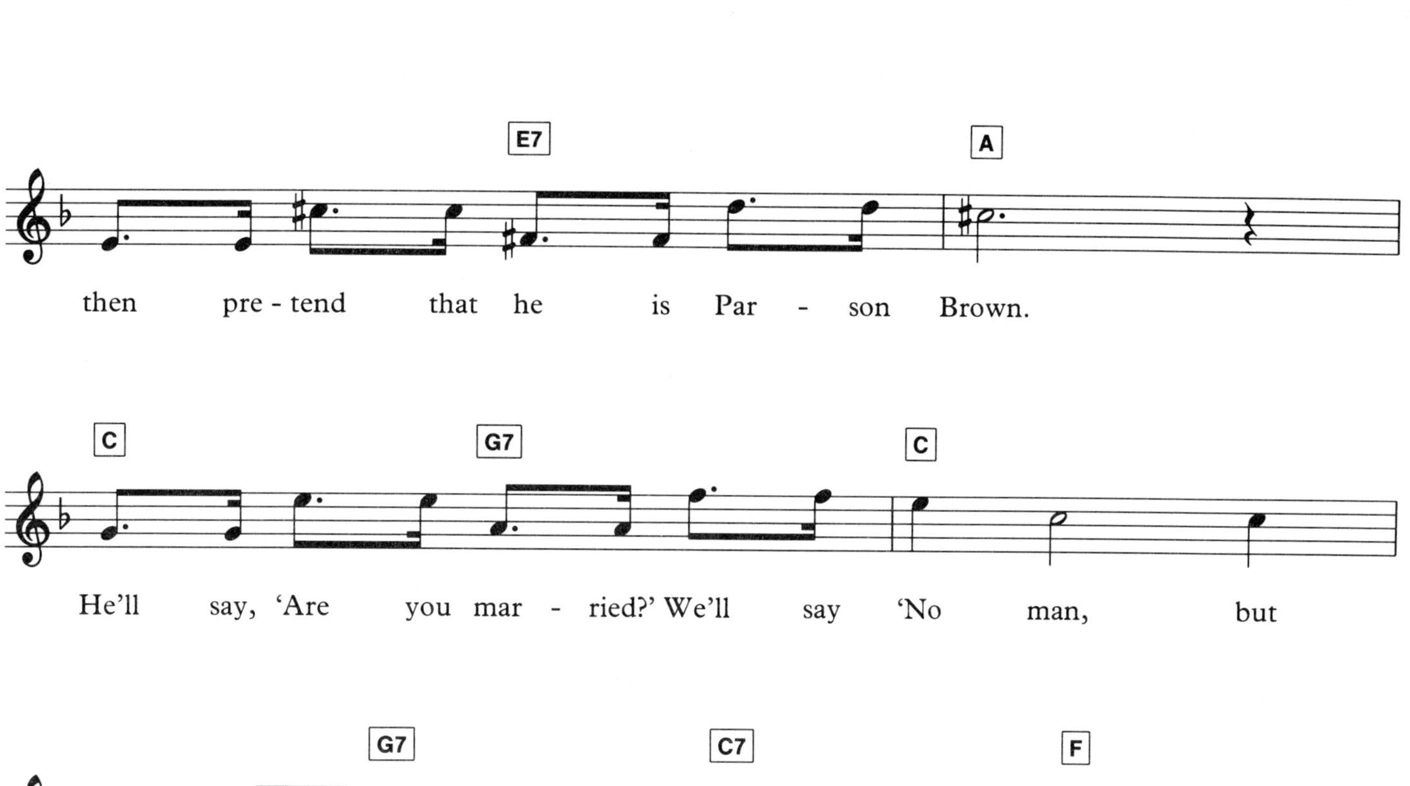
E7
A
then pre - tend that he is Par - son Brown.

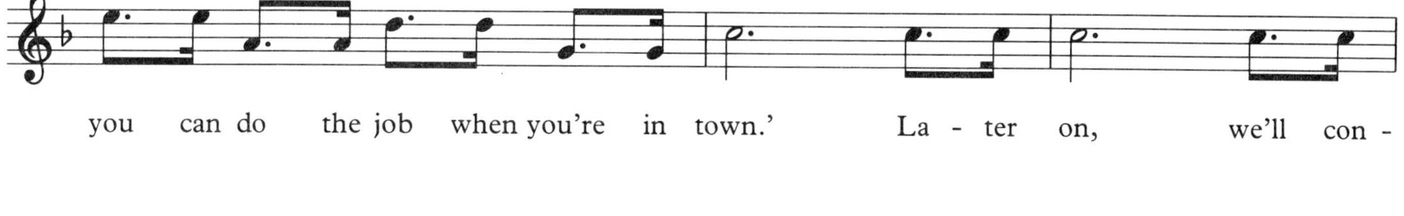
C
G7
C
He'll say, 'Are you mar - ried?' We'll say 'No man, but

G7
C7
F
you can do the job when you're in town.' La - ter on, we'll con -

C7
-spi - re, as we dream by the fi - re, to face un-a - fraid the

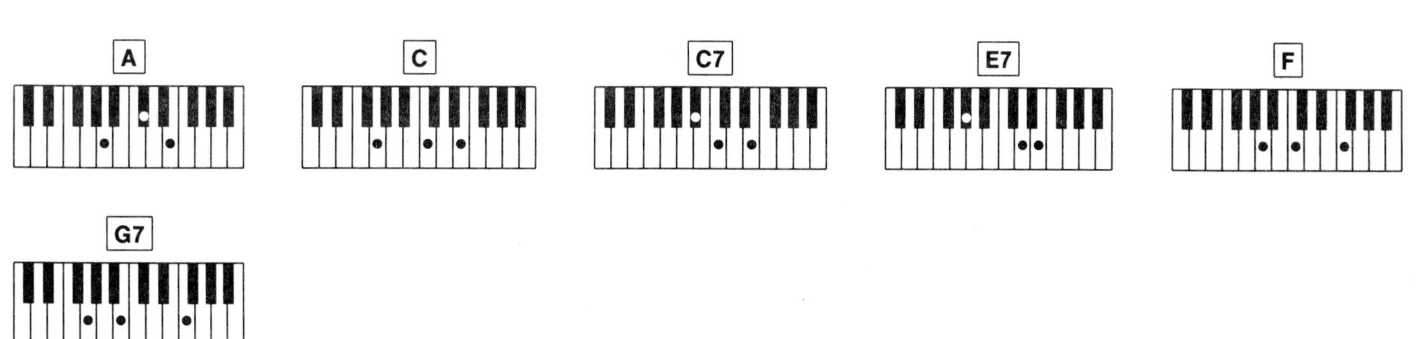
F
plans that we made, walk - ing in a win - ter won - der - land.

A
C
C7
E7
F
G7

The Easy Keyboard Library Series

Big Band Hits
Order Ref: 19098

Popular Classics
Order Ref: 4180A

Blues
Order Ref: 3477A

Pub Singalong Collection
Order Ref: 3954A

Celebration Songs
Order Ref: 3478A

Rock 'n' Roll Classics
Order Ref: 2224A

Christmas Carols
Order Ref: 4616A

Traditional Scottish Favourites
Order Ref: 4231A

Christmas Songs
Order Ref: 19198

Showtunes - Volume 1
Order Ref: 19103

Classic Hits - Volume 1
Order Ref: 19099

Showtunes - Volume 2
Order Ref: 3328A

Classic Hits - Volume 2
Order Ref: 19100

Soft Rock Collection
Order Ref: 4617A

Country Songs
Order Ref: 19101

Soul Classics
Order Ref: 19201

Traditional English Favourites
Order Ref: 4229A

Summer Collection
Order Ref: 3489A

Favourite Hymns
Order Ref: 4179A

TV Themes
Order Ref: 19196

Film Classics
Order Ref: 19197

The Twenties
Order Ref: 2969A

Great Songwriters
Order Ref: 2225A

The Thirties
Order Ref: 2970A

Instrumental Classics
Order Ref: 2338A

The Forties
Order Ref: 2971A

Traditional Irish Favourites
Order Ref: 4230A

The Fifties
Order Ref: 2972A

Love Songs - Volume 1
Order Ref: 19102

The Sixties
Order Ref: 2973A

Love Songs - Volume 2
Order Ref: 19199

The Seventies
Order Ref: 2974A

Music Hall
Order Ref: 3329A

The Eighties
Order Ref: 2975A

Motown Classics
Order Ref: 2337A

The Nineties
Order Ref: 2976A

Number One Hits
Order Ref: 19200

Wartime Collection
Order Ref: 3955A

Wedding Collection
Order Ref: 3688A

Exclusive distributors:

International Music Publications Limited
Southend Road, Woodford Green, Essex IG8 8HN
International Music Publications Limited
25 Rue D'Hauteville, 75010 Paris, France
International Music Publications GmbH Germany
Marstallstrasse 8, D-80539 München, Germany
Nuova Carisch S.R.L.
Via M.F. Quintiliano 40, 20138 Milano, Italy
Danmusik
Vognmagergade 7, DK-1120 Copenhagen K, Denmark